Docs-as-Ecosystem

The Community Approach to Engineering Documentation

Alejandra Quetzalli

Apress®

Docs-as-Ecosystem: The Community Approach to Engineering Documentation

Alejandra Quetzalli
Seattle, WA, USA

ISBN-13 (pbk): 978-1-4842-9327-0   ISBN-13 (electronic): 978-1-4842-9328-7
https://doi.org/10.1007/978-1-4842-9328-7

Managing Director, Apress Media LLC: Welmoed Spahr
Acquisitions Editor: Shiva Ramachandran
Development Editor: James Markham
Coordinating Editor: Mark Powers

Cover designed by eStudioCalamar

Distributed to the book trade worldwide by Apress Media, LLC, 1 New York Plaza, New York, NY 10004, U.S.A. Phone 1-800-SPRINGER, fax (201) 348-4505, e-mail orders-ny@springer-sbm.com, or visit www.springeronline.com. Apress Media, LLC is a California LLC and the sole member (owner) is Springer Science + Business Media Finance Inc (SSBM Finance Inc). SSBM Finance Inc is a **Delaware** corporation.

For information on translations, please e-mail booktranslations@springernature.com; for reprint, paperback, or audio rights, please e-mail bookpermissions@springernature.com.

Apress titles may be purchased in bulk for academic, corporate, or promotional use. eBook versions and licenses are also available for most titles. For more information, reference our Print and eBook Bulk Sales web page at http://www.apress.com/bulk-sales.

Any source code or other supplementary material referenced by the author in this book is available to readers on GitHub (https://github.com/Apress). For more detailed information, please visit http://www.apress.com/source-code.

Paper in this product is recyclable

This book is dedicated to all the dogs in the world whose loyal companionship to their family units reminds us of the importance of giving back to our communities. Dogs are one of the best parts of our ecosystem; they help maintain balance, provide support, and bring life to even the bleakest of places. Dogs teach us valuable lessons about interdependent relationships and caring for our communities. They show us that growth only comes when you're willing to put your ego last and work collaboratively toward a common goal. Thank you, majestic companions, for being an integral part of our ecosystems and reminding us of the importance of building and nurturing strong communities.

Table of Contents

About the Author

 **Alejandra Quetzalli** is a Latina from México with ten years of experience in the tech industry and has a devoted autism service dog, Canela. Canela works side by side with Alejandra, even joining her traveling and speaking engagements at tech conferences worldwide. Throughout her career, Alejandra has worked in SEO, paid search, full-stack development, UX, developer relations, technical writing (engineering documentation), AWS cloud advocacy, startups, and Open Source Software (OSS). She's currently a core maintainer at AsyncAPI Initiative, leading OSS initiatives for AsyncAPI Docs and Education. In 2022, she became a member of the AsyncAPI Technical Steering Committee (TSC).

In 2016, she founded sheCodesNow.org to provide accessible programming workshops for women and minorities transitioning into tech. Today, sheCodesNow has grown to develop technical courses in technical writing, developer relations, and tech community building.

About the Technical Reviewer

 **Vidushi Meel** has worked on documentation as a freelancer and employee at various AI companies, such as Viso AI and Snorkel AI. She's published three iOS apps and a research paper on skin cancer detection with AI in 2022.

Acknowledgments

I want to take a moment to express my gratitude to the many individuals who helped make this book possible.

I want to give a special shoutout to my service dog, Canela, who always reminds me that there's a world beyond my laptop screen. She thinks I should spend less time writing about docs-as-ecosystem and more time training together for our next agility round. I'm thankful she pushes me to work out daily and live in the present moment.

To cool Uncle Larry, who shares my love of dog family members and welcomes my idiosyncrasies; thank you for being in my life.

I am grateful to Shiva, my acquisition editor, who believed in my vision and gave me my first opportunity to publish. Your wise guidance and support, even when I made last-minute changes to the title, were invaluable.

To Mark Powers, thank you for your patience during my many writer's block rounds. Your persistence kept me on track, even when I felt overwhelmed and exhausted. I'm convinced that you must have answered a million and one questions from me. At this point, you probably know more about my book than I do!

Suzie Miller, thank you for sharing your expertise by providing a wealth of resources and information on accessibility for Chapter 1.

Last but not least, a heartfelt thanks to the entire community of documentation enthusiasts who have supported and even promoted my docs-as-ecosystem model. Our shared passion for improving documentation and nurturing ongoing conversations with communities is my source of inspiration.

ACKNOWLEDGMENTS

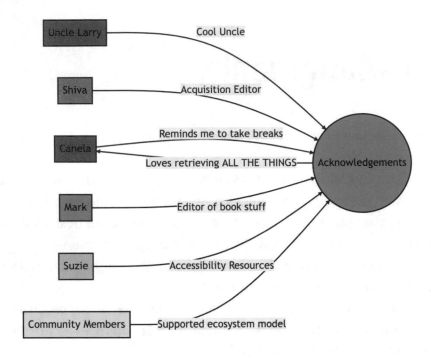

Endorsements

I've found my new go-to reference for all things documentation. This book provides a fresh perspective on docs and why treating them as an ecosystem is so vital. Not only does it cover the documentation process, but it also delves into the critical aspects of SEO, accessibility, UX/UI design, and more. Its comprehensive approach and wealth of helpful knowledge really set this book apart. Whether you're a technical writer, product manager, or OSS contributor, this book is an essential guide to mastering documentation.

—Kurt Kemple (Sr. Director, Developer Growth and Engagement, Slack)

My dear and esteemed colleague Alejandra Quetzalli is proposing the approach of treating technical documentation as an ecosystem and is writing a book about it. I completely agree with this approach. In order for documentation to be useful (which involves being correct, accessible, extendable, searchable, up to date, and many more things), we need to manage it as an ecosystem.

—Pedro Galván (Head of Content and Technology, Software Guru)

As a Documentation Engineer, I firmly believe that documentation is an essential part of software development, and adopting a "docs-as-ecosystem" approach can benefit the entire tech community, regardless of skill level. The "docs-as-ecosystem" approach emphasizes the importance of documentation throughout the software development life cycle, creating an inclusive and collaborative way of creating and maintaining documentation. By prioritizing documentation, developers can improve the usability, maintainability, and scalability of software products, making it easier for everyone to build upon and contribute to them. Alejandra's approach to "docs-as-ecosystem" fosters a culture of learning and knowledge sharing, making it easier for beginners to learn from more experienced developers and quickly become proficient in the industry. I believe that adopting a "docs-as-ecosystem" approach is a critical step toward creating a more inclusive and supportive tech community that encourages growth, innovation, and collaboration.

—Brittney Ball (Documentation Engineer, Meta, Featured in NYT)

One new approach to accessible documentation I'm excited to learn more about has been created by the amazing Alejandra Quetzalli known as docs-as-ecosystem, which builds on the concept of docs-as-code.

I'm especially taken by her approach to the importance of retrieving and incorporating community feedback. Alejandra says, "The term docs-as-ecosystem highlights the importance of retrieving and integrating community feedback in documentation development. It recognizes that documentation is about providing information and meeting community needs and preferences."

I believe this strongly, too, especially around it being everyone's job to make sure content is accessible for all, which doesn't just mean colors or fonts, but "are acronyms defined?", "is the content clear to all levels of the audience?", etc. There is nothing worse than trying to decode bad documentation in an outage or time-limited situation.

—Suzie Miller (Senior Cloud Solutions Architect, Microsoft, Featured in "Disability Power 100 List UK Influencer 2021")

Preface: Why Docs-as-Ecosystem?

Dear community member,

As you hold this book in your hands, I want to thank you for taking an interest in my new approach to engineering documentation, the **docs-as-ecosystem** model. In these pages, you'll find a heartfelt guide to implementing this model in your documentation processes and why it benefits our communities.

The current global pandemic highlights the importance of building and giving back to our communities. As technical writers, we are no strangers to the isolation that comes with working remotely or drowning in engineering workflows and processes. But it's 2023, and we must do better. Technical writers shouldn't be relegated to working in silos, detached from the diverse stakeholders that enrich documentation work.

For me, the word "community" carries a special meaning as a Latina. In my Mexican and Latin American culture, community is not just a group of people living in the same area, but a supportive network of individuals that take care of each other. I believe this sense of community should be applied to our work as technical writers, as we build ecosystems of community feedback to shape and grow our engineering documentation.

At the same time, I'm also acutely aware of the echoing silence that often greets me after I vocalize issues related to disability. As a disabled community member, it can be disheartening to see people ghost me or disengage when I bring up topics that make them uncomfortable. I believe we can do better as a community, and that starts with embracing vulnerability and discomfort in order to grow.

In this book, I hope to introduce a new way of thinking about engineering documentation: the ecosystem approach. Just like how an ecosystem in nature is made up of diverse species working together to sustain life, a thriving documentation ecosystem relies on a diverse group of contributors working together to create and maintain high-quality documentation. Through this lens, I hope to help technical writers and their stakeholders understand the value of collaboration so that we can create documentation that is accessible, inclusive, and meaningful to all.

How Docs-as-Ecosystem Was Born

My approach to engineering documentation inspired me to coin a new term, **docs-as-ecosystem**. The word *ecosystem* promotes a paradigm where community members treat documentation as a complex and dynamic system that must be managed and nurtured. I came to this model after ten years of experience as a technical writer, observing the limitations of traditional approaches to engineering documentation.

Initially, I saw documentation as a static product to be created and delivered for engineers. *(In fact, this book was originally going to be titled* Designing Developer Documentation as a Product*!)* But over time, I realized this approach was limiting and didn't truly capture documentation's educational value in global communities. My thinking evolved, and I began to see documentation as an ecosystem, a conversation between diverse documentation creators and multiple community stakeholders. One day, I realized that what I actually believed was that the docs conversation is a dynamic and ongoing exchange of ideas, feedback, and insights between global documentation creators and community members.

Let's summarize a few reasons for community members to adopt the "docs-as-ecosystem" model:

1. **Proposes a more holistic and community-centered approach**: The term "docs-as-ecosystem" recognizes that documentation is not just a set of Markdown files or code snippets but an ecosystem that needs to be managed and nurtured. The term "docs-as-code" has been widely adopted recently, but it may not fully capture the complexity and diversity of documentation development. The term "docs-as-ecosystem" aligns with the industry trend toward a more holistic and community-centered approach to documentation development.

2. **Encourages collaboration**: The term "docs-as-ecosystem" acknowledges that documentation development involves different roles and stakeholders, such as technical writers, designers, developers, community members, and beyond. By adopting this term, the software developer community can encourage collaboration across diverse stakeholders and facilitate the creation of high-quality documentation.

3. **Emphasizes the importance of retrieving and incorporating community feedback**: The term "docs-as-ecosystem" highlights the importance of retrieving and integrating community feedback in documentation development. It recognizes that documentation is about providing information and meeting community needs and preferences.

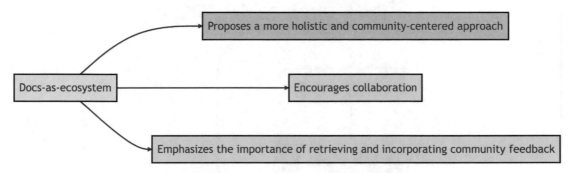

Figure 1. *Three reasons to adopt the docs-as-ecosystem model*

The Docs-as-Ecosystem Model Starts and Ends with Community Feedback

The **docs-as-ecosystem** model starts with **community feedback**, captured through various channels such as *public GitHub discussions, public surveys, forums, social media,* and *support requests*. This feedback is then incorporated into the documentation code base, which is managed through **version control** to ensure that all changes are tracked and reviewed.

The documentation code base is then **integrated continuously** through a continuous integration process, which helps catch errors and ensure that documentation updates are consistent with the rest of the code base. The code base is then used to **generate static site documentation**, the basis for the final **generated documentation**.

The generated documentation is then **published** to a production environment, where it's accessible to the community. Finally, the community can **review the results and provide updated feedback on the published documentation**, which starts the cycle anew.

Incorporating community feedback ensures documentation remains up to date and accurate, reflecting the needs and concerns of the community. Building stronger relationships between community and documentation creation processes leads to engaged and thriving communities.

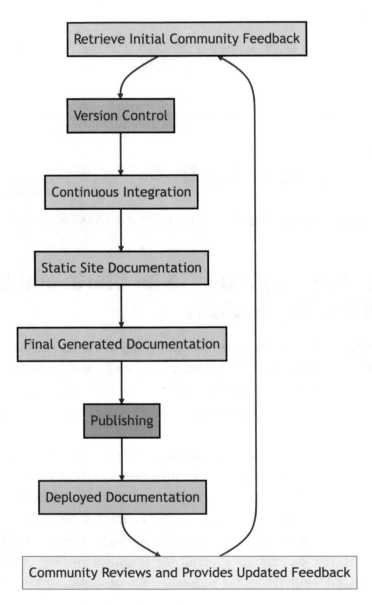

Figure 2. *The diverse stakeholders and collaborators involved in providing* ***community feedback and review***

This diagram shows the diverse stakeholders and collaborators involved in providing **community feedback and review**, captured through various channels such as *events, social media, email, Slack, Discord, public GitHub discussions, public surveys, forums, support requests, etc.*

Developer relations play a key role in collecting and analyzing this feedback, helping to identify trends and insights that can be used to improve the documentation.

Technical writers are responsible for incorporating community feedback into the documentation code base, using feedback from various sources, including *public GitHub discussions, social media*, and *feedback from engineers, product managers, OSS community members*, etc.

In the enterprise world, **product managers** help guide the direction of the documentation, ensuring that it meets the target audience's needs and reflects the product road map.

In the OSS world, **OSS community members** are a critical part of the documentation process, providing feedback, suggestions, and contributions to the documentation code base.

Engineers are responsible for building and maintaining the product itself and play an important role in ensuring that the documentation accurately reflects the functionality and capabilities of the product.

Customer support and account managers can provide unique feedback and insights from customer interactions, even **sales**.

Students may also be involved in the documentation process, contributing ideas and insights from their unique perspectives.

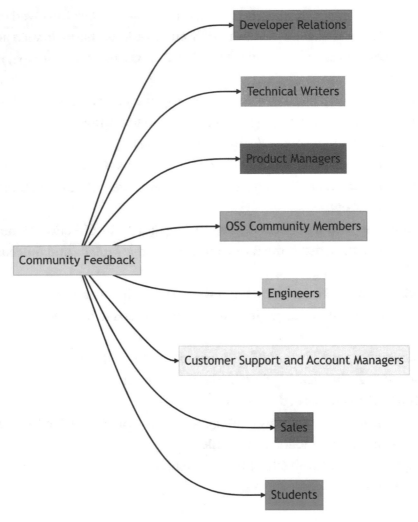

Figure 3. *The diverse stakeholders involved in community feedback and review, highlighting the importance of collaboration and communication across different roles and functions to create effective and community-friendly documentation*

Why "Community" Is More Representative Than "Users"

In the traditional software development model, we're used to writing engineering documentation with a specific user in mind. However, this approach can be limiting because it assumes a single "ideal" user represents your entire user base.

The docs-as-ecosystem model proposes a different way of thinking about engineering documentation; it recognizes docs aren't simply a static product but an ongoing conversation between diverse documentation creators (contributors) and community members.

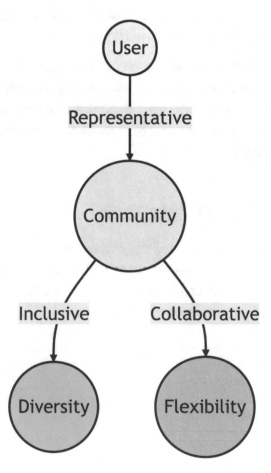

Figure 4. *Why "community" is more representative than "users"*

Thinking in terms of community instead of users is more

1. **Inclusive**: Focusing on the community is more inclusive than focusing only on users because it recognizes that many different types of stakeholders contribute to and read the documentation.

2. **Diverse**: Focusing on the community encourages diversity and inclusion because it recognizes many different backgrounds and experiences.

3. **Collaborative**: Focusing on the community also fosters a more collaborative approach to documentation because it encourages anyone from any background to participate.

By focusing on community, the docs-as-ecosystem approach offers a more flexible, adaptable, and sustainable way to approach engineering documentation. Rather than assuming that there is a single "ideal" user, we recognize that engineering documentation is a dynamic and ongoing conversation between documentation creators and the community.

Onward, Community Members

Throughout this book, you'll find colorful diagrams of the docs-as-ecosystem model, showcasing how to apply it to real-world scenarios. I hope you find this approach inspiring and compelling. Thank you for joining me on this journey, where we seek more collaborative, community-centric documentation.

CHAPTER 1

Accessibility

In this chapter, I will introduce the subject of *Accessibility*.

My first goal is to help you understand the importance of accessibility in engineering documentation. By prioritizing accessibility, you can reach a wider audience and increase your revenue potential. My second goal is to equip you with the necessary tools to conduct thorough accessibility audits on your documentation. By the end of this chapter, you should feel confident in your ability to identify and address accessibility issues in your documentation, and continue to improve your accessibility best practices.

Figure 1-1 illustrates different disabilities and impairments that can affect community members using your documentation.

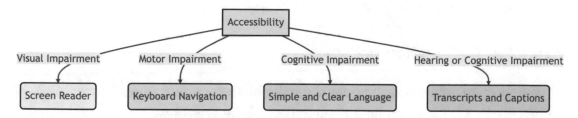

Figure 1-1. *Different disabilities and impairments that can affect users and how to design documentation to accommodate each one*

Why the Need?

According to the Centers for Disease Control and Prevention (CDC), *in the United States alone*, **26% (one in four)** of adults have some type of disability.[1] Figure 1-2 illustrates the following statistics:

- **13.7%** of people have a **mobility disability**.

- **10.8%** of people have a **cognitive disability**.

---

[1] www.cdc.gov/ncbddd/disabilityandhealth/infographic-disability-impacts-all.html

© Alejandra Quetzalli 2023
A. Quetzalli, *Docs-as-Ecosystem*, https://doi.org/10.1007/978-1-4842-9328-7_1

- **6.8%** of people have an **independent living disability**.

- **5.9%** of people have a **hearing disability**.

- **4.6%** of people have a **vision disability**.

- **3.7%** of people have a **self-care disability**.

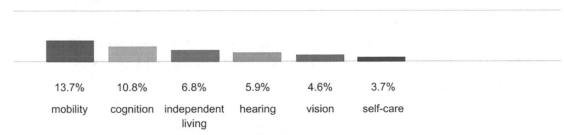

Figure 1-2. *CDC disability statistics*

People often hold misconceptions about disabilities and their impact on daily life, leading to a lack of understanding about the need for accessibility.

While many may think that accessibility is just about caring for the disabled, it's also about ensuring you are not losing up to 26% of additional revenue by neglecting a significant segment of your customer base.

Figure 1-3 visually illustrates the potential losses in customers and revenue that come with not producing accessible products.

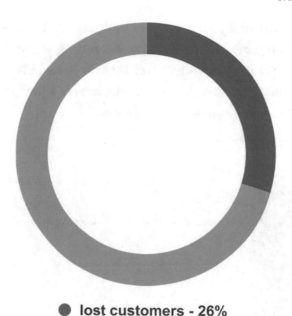

● **lost customers - 26%**

Figure 1-3. *Potential losses in customers and revenue*

To put this revenue loss into perspective, consider a business that sold 225,000 backpack units at an average price of $25 per unit, resulting in total annual revenue of $5,625,000. Figure 1-4 shows the mentioned backpacks for sale. With 26% of the adult population having a disability, that business could have had a total revenue of up to $7,087,500.

Figure 1-4. *Sample backpacks for sale*

Inclusive design can actually increase your bottom line, as shown in Figure 1-5. By investing in making your products and websites accessible, you not only generate more revenue but also make the world a better place for everyone. This chapter will delve into best practices for conducting an accessibility audit, but it's equally important to first understand the tangible benefits of inclusive design.

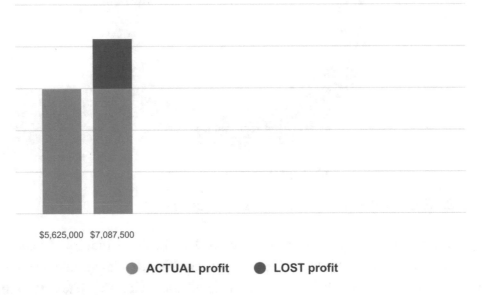

Figure 1-5. *Actual profit vs. potential lost profit*

By not considering accessibility, businesses may be limiting their customer base and revenue potential. However, it is important to note that the actual percentage of revenue impact for accessibility issues varies depending on your specific business and product/service offerings.

Where Does Accessibility Begin for Docs?

Accessibility practices are not a one-time deal but rather a continuous effort to ensure equal access for everyone. Let's delve into practical steps for incorporating accessibility best practices into your documentation creation process, including techniques for testing your site against the diverse success criteria from Web Content Accessibility Guidelines (WCAG) and W3C. Figure 1-6 highlights some of the steps for incorporating accessibility that we'll cover in this chapter.

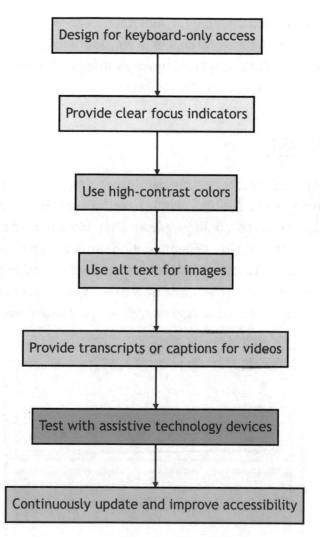

Figure 1-6. *Steps to ensure accessibility in documentation*

W3C (*World Wide Web Consortium*) is an international community that develops and promotes web standards. It develops technical specifications and guidelines for the Web, including accessibility guidelines. **WCAG** (*Web Content Accessibility Guidelines*) is a set of guidelines developed by W3C to make web content more accessible to people with disabilities. WCAG provides a standard for web content accessibility recognized and adopted by governments and organizations worldwide. Essentially, W3C is an organization that develops and promotes web standards, while WCAG is a set of guidelines for web content accessibility developed by W3C.

It's important to note that this chapter does not cover every aspect of accessibility, as there are numerous guidelines and checks to consider. However, we will address the most common and impactful issues faced by community members in this field.

May the winds of progress be ever in our favor!

Semantic HTML

Semantic HTML is HTML tags that give semantic meaning to web pages. It's good for screen readers and physically disabled people because using HTML elements for their given purpose makes it easier for both people and machines to read and understand it. Using the correct HTML tags in a documentation site is a big part of keeping your documentation accessible. This section is devoted to teaching the importance of several semantic HTML tags, how to use them, and how to test your site for accessibility. Figure 1-7 illustrates semantic HTML tags on a web page: header, nav, article, img, and footer.

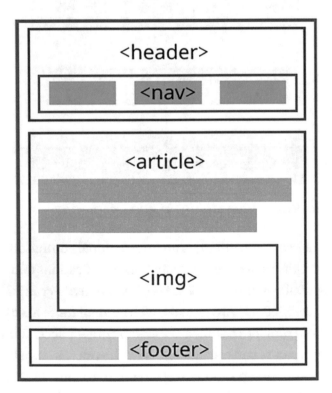

Figure 1-7. *Semantic HTML tags on a web page: header, nav, article, img, and footer*

Ambiguous or Incomplete Anchor Text

A link is incomplete and/or ambiguous if a user has to read the surrounding copy around the link to get an idea of where it could take them.

```
<a href="url">Read More</a>
```

Here are some examples of ambiguous anchor text:

- Learn More
- Read More
- Click Here
- Go Here
- Here
- More
- Continue
- Keep Reading
- Sign up

If a user is reliant on a screen reader, it's vital that each button has informative text that stands on its own. Because users reliant on screen readers navigate a web page differently than people who can use a mouse and computer screen, you cannot assume that they will easily figure out the context surrounding each Call-to-Action (CTA) button.

Figure 1-8 illustrates how an HTML button that only says "Read More" isn't informative in isolation; you're forced to read the surrounding copy and headings in order to figure out where the link takes you.

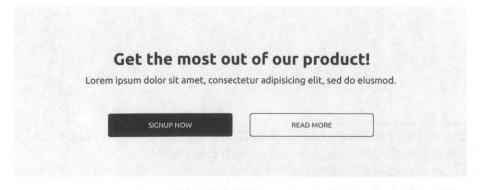

Figure 1-8. *A website page with an HTML button that only says "Read More"*

Check out the success criteria that WCAG 2.1 provides for anchor text:

"The purpose of each link can be determined from the link text alone or from the link text together with its programmatically determined link context, except where the purpose of the link would be ambiguous to users in general."[2]

Blinking or Flashing Content

A flash is a rapidly changing image sequence generating HTML elements with blinking properties that are set at a predetermined rate. A blink is elements switching back and forth between two visual states. While <blink> is a deprecated feature in HTML, flashing content can still be found across the web. But did you know that flashing content may cause seizures or strong physical reactions to some people? With this in mind, it should be no surprise to hear that adding blinking or flashing content doesn't pass the WCAG 2.1 success criterion.[3]

```
<blink>So don't do this.</blink>

<span style="text-decoration:blink">Or this.</span.
```

More specifically, WCAG 2.1 states that there should be "no more than three **general flashes** and/or no more than three **red flashes** within any one-second period."[4]

While you might be tempted to disable flashing or blinking behavior in your HTML, CSS, or scripts, it's not a viable solution. These types of animations are not supported on assistive technologies such as screen readers,[5] making your content inaccessible to a significant portion of your audience. Figure 1-9 illustrates diverse types of flashing content that shouldn't be used in documentation.

---

[2] WCAG 2.1 Link Purpose success criteria: www.w3.org/TR/WCAG21/#link-purpose-in-context

[3] www.w3.org/TR/WCAG21/#seizures-and-physical-reactions

[4] www.w3.org/TR/WCAG21/#dfn-flashes

[5] www.w3.org/TR/2008/WD-WCAG20-TECHS-20080430/F4.html

NO FLASHING CONTENT ALLOWED

Figure 1-9. *No flashing content should be allowed on your web pages*

Instead, let's prioritize the accessibility of our engineering documentation site by avoiding flashing GIFs, elements, or animations. By doing so, we ensure everyone, including visual designers, can access and benefit from our content.

Color-Blind-Friendly Palettes

Color-blind-friendly palettes impact accessibility because color plays a significant role in data visualizations and engineering diagrams. Colors highlight important information and illustrate relationships between various types of data. If the colors selected for your data visualizations or engineering diagrams are not color-blind-friendly palettes, you're creating content that won't help a big chunk of your readers.

According to the *Colour Blind Awareness*[6] organization, color blindness affects 1 in 12 men (8%) and 1 in 200 women (0.5%). Worldwide, they calculated that there are an estimated 300 million color-blind people!

Being color blind means that one or more types of cone cells (cells that detect color) in a person's eyes aren't working and are producing a reduced color space. For example, two colors that look different to someone with normal color vision may appear to be the same color to someone who is color blind.

Figure 1-10 illustrates the three main types of color blindness:

- **Protanopia**: Known as "red weakness," this type of red/green color blindness affects people who are unable to perceive red light.

- **Deuteranopia/deuteranomaly**: Known as "green weakness," this type of red/green color blindness affects people who are *insensitive* to green light (deuteranomaly) or are *unable to perceive* green light (deuteranopia).

- **Tritanopia**: Known as "yellow weakness," this type of blue/yellow color blindness affects people who have difficulty distinguishing between blue and yellow colors.

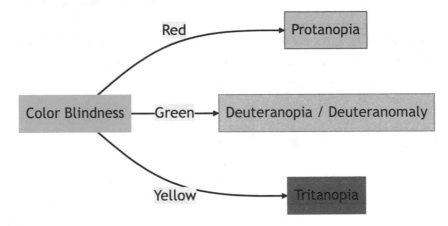

Figure 1-10. *Types of color blindness*

Choose wisely which colors you select to tell your data's story. To learn more about what WCAG says, check out their article on "Use of Color."[7]

---

[6] www.colourblindawareness.org/colour-blindness/

[7] www.w3.org/WAI/WCAG21/Understanding/use-of-color.html

Duplicate Alt-Text

Writing duplicate alt-text or captions for two images that are identical affects accessibility because people who cannot see the images will think that they are the same.

Let's take a look at Figure 1-11 that illustrates sample duplicate alt-text.

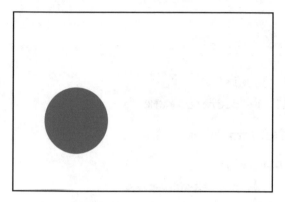
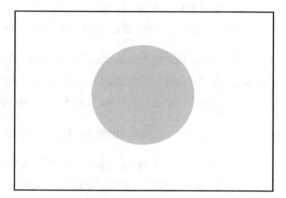

Sample Duplicate Alt-text: "image of a circle"

Sample Duplicate Alt-text: "image of a circle"

Figure 1-11. *Sample duplicate alt-text: "image of a circle"*

Now imagine if you simply wrote in the caption or alt-text for both of those images that it's a circle. That wouldn't be helpful at all because you didn't take the time to distinguish the little differences between the two images such as the **placement** of the circles, their **size** differences, and **color** differences!

Figure 1-12 illustrates the accessible approach with corrected alt-text.

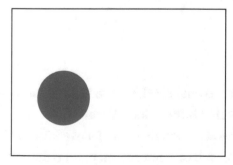
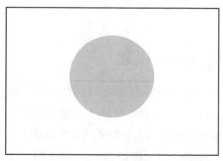

Sample Duplicate Alt-text: "image of a small and light purple circle in the bottom left corner"

Sample Duplicate Alt-text: "image of a large mint green circle in the center"

Figure 1-12. *The accessible approach with corrected alt-text*

Duplicate Form Label

Using duplicate form labels impacts accessibility because it confuses screen readers, resulting in some screen readers only being able to read **one** of the duplicate form labels. Can you imagine how confusing it becomes for users reliant on screen reader technology to navigate inconsistent forms?

Here's an example of duplicate form labels:

```
<label for="preferredname2">Name</label>
<label for="preferredname2">Preferred:</label>
<input type="text" name="preferredname" id="preferredname2">
```

Let's clean it up and remove duplicate HTML form labels:

```
<label for="preferredname2">Preferred Name:</label>
<input type="text" name="preferredname" id="preferredname2">
```

If we see what WCAG thinks about the matter, their website points out[8] the following guideline of what labels should provide to all users:

> *3.3.2 Labels or Instructions, Level A: Labels or instructions are provided when content requires user input.*

This matters because in a screen reader, labels are needed to identify the controls in a form so that users know what input data is expected. If their screen reader cannot read all labels without confusion, then the disabled user is blocked from completing a successful form.

Empty Buttons

Using an empty button or an anchor link in place of an HTML button impacts accessibility because screen readers won't understand what that button does. When you don't specify a value, you produce an **empty button** that confuses screen readers. If a user doesn't know what your button is for because they cannot access it on their screen reader, then they won't be able to interact with it! Even worse, if they did somehow manage to instead trigger it via their mouse or a keyboard event, they might get unexpected results.

---

[8]www.w3.org/WAI/WCAG21/Understanding/labels-or-instructions.html

If you are unfamiliar with the error message related to empty HTML buttons, you may initially wonder who would make such a mistake. However, you would be surprised at the mistakes people make! To give you a better understanding, let's examine the following empty button code snippet sample and explain why it fails an accessibility test:

```
<div>
    <button>
        <span class="button subscribeEmail"></span>
        <img src="https://mywebsite.com/assets/subcribeEmailButton.jgp"
        alt="subscribe email">
    </button>
</div>
```

Why use an image and try to link out by forcing in an anchor link or image link? Not only is it messy code, but this image doesn't provide an input or value attribute for a screen reader to click through.

Instead, do this:

```
<div>
    <button aria-label="subscribe email button" title="subscribe email
    button">
        <span aria-hidden="true" class="subscribeEmail"></span>
    </button>
</div>
```

Here's another important example showcasing what **not** to do in the wild:

```
<button type="submit">
    <svg id="search" viewBox="0 0 13 22.3">
        <path d="P64, 15.7L12.0,22A17.8,3.7,13, 9.2,27,6.7C3"></path>
    </svg>
</button>
```

This second example would also get flagged with the accessibility error of empty button because the only content inside of our search bar's submit button is an inline SVG that has **no content or alt-text**. How can a screen reader read this button? (Hint: they can't!)

Instead, let's write cleaner CSS code by saving the SVG as an image and adding alt-text:

```
<button type="submit">
    <img src="/search-bar.svg" alt="Search"/>
</button>
```

To learn more about what WCAG dictates regarding Empty Buttons, check out their article "Button has non-empty accessible name."[9]

Empty Heading Tag

Using an Empty Heading Tag impacts accessibility because if a user is navigating the contents of the page with a screen reader and they encounter an empty heading, they may move forward to the next heading in the list, potentially missing entire sections of content.

Empty Heading Tags often happen by pure accident. Sometimes, a developer will accidentally open a tag and their IDE or tool of choice autocompletes the tag for them without them realizing. Regardless of how these mistakes make it to production, it's important we correct them once we spot them.

The best way to solve an Empty Heading Tag is to comb through your code and fill out empty headings or delete unnecessary ones.

Here's an example of an Empty Heading Tag that needs to be corrected:

```
<h3></h3>
```

Here's an example of a useful and helpful heading:

```
<h3>Fix Accessibility Issues</h3>
```

If you're curious to see what WCAG has to say about this, check out their article on Success Criterion for Headings and Labels.[10]

---

[9] Accessible Buttons: www.w3.org/WAI/standards-guidelines/act/rules/
button-non-empty-accessible-name-97a4e1/

[10] Success Criterion for Headings and Labels: www.w3.org/WAI/WCAG21/Understanding/
headings-and-labels

Empty Link

Similar to the Empty Heading Tag scenario, sometimes, Empty Links are also accidentally released to production! Empty Links impact accessibility because they don't show a screen reader where a link goes when clicked or triggered.

You may be thinking this issue happens when a developer accidentally leaves an empty anchor link or two in your code. But rather, a more appropriate example for this scenario is social media buttons! When a social media button is coded with Font Awesome icons but no alt-text is added, the Empty Link error will be flagged during your accessibility testing.

Here's an example of an incorrect Empty Link:

```
<a href="https://twitter.com/yourBusinessTwitterHandle">
    <i class="fa fa-twitter"></i>
</a>
```

Remember to always add alt-text and/or a title to all links, especially to social media buttons! Since you cannot add alt-text to font icons like Font Awesome, we will fix our previous code snippet and make it pass the accessibility test by adding an Aria label.

Let's fix our previous code by adding the following Aria label:

```
<a href="https://twitter.com/yourBusinessTwitterHandle" aria-label="My Business Name's Twitter">
    <i class="fa fa-twitter"></i>
</a>
```

If you'd like to learn more about this specific Font Awesome use case, Font Awesome has nice documentation about how to use their icons with accessibility in mind.[11]

If you'd like to see what WCAG has to say about Empty Links, check out their article on measuring the success criterion for non-text content.[12]

---

[11] https://fontawesome.com/v4.7/accessibility/

[12] www.w3.org/TR/WCAG21/#non-text-content

Empty or Missing Table Header

Empty or missing table headers impact accessibility because they block screen readers from being able to interpret data in a table and show the relationship between table cells. Tables with filled-out table headers allow screen readers to read an entire row/column all at once or to navigate tables one cell at a time. Imagine a really big table and how awful it would feel to be blocked from fully understanding all of the information contained in the table! Moving forward, remember to never leave an empty <th> in your tables and that each <td> should have a corresponding <th>.

Here's an example of how to properly include correlating <th> tags in your tables:

```
<table>
<thead>
  <tr>
      <th>Dog</th>
      <th>Age</th>
      <th>Gender</th>
  </tr>
</thead>
<tbody>
  <tr>
      <td>Canela</td>
      <td>3</td>
      <td>Female</td>
  </tr>
  <tr>
      <td>Ink</td>
      <td>7</td>
      <td>Male</td>
  </tr>
  <tr>
      <td>Spot</td>
      <td>1</td>
      <td>Male</td>
  </tr>
 </tbody>
</table>
```

If you'd like to learn more about what WCAG says on empty or missing table headers, check out their article on "Understanding Info and Relationships."[13]

Image Missing Alternative Text

Image Missing Alternative Text impacts accessibility because people who rely on screen reader technology rely on alt-text to get an idea of what the image represents. When alt-text is completely missing from an image, the visual and contextual way of learning is lost. Think of engineering diagrams and how much information they help present to explain a data story over time or to explain how a certain piece of a technology works.

To learn more about the success criterion from WCAG on non-text content, check out the section on non-text content in their article.[14]

Incorrect Heading Order

Incorrect Heading Order impacts accessibility because skipping over a heading level breaks the semantic structure by which we should be creating our web pages.

If you'd like to see more about what passes the WCAG success criterion for headings and the structure they bring to web pages, check out the following article: `www.w3.org/WAI/WCAG21/Understanding/headings-and-labels.html`.

Insufficient Color Contrast

Insufficient Color Contrast impacts accessibility because without adequate color contrast, users will find it hard to read text in images, slides, videos, etc. This is particularly hard for users with low vision and color blindness.

To learn more about the **minimum** success criterion required for color contrast from WCAG, check out the following article: `www.w3.org/TR/WCAG21/#contrast-minimum`.

---

[13] `www.w3.org/WAI/WCAG21/Understanding/info-and-relationships.html`
[14] `www.w3.org/TR/WCAG21/#non-text-content`

Missing Language Declaration

Missing Language Declaration impacts accessibility because it blocks assistive devices from identifying what language a web page is written in and users who require assistive devices to access site content.

Screen readers need these language attributes to read the content of a page; without an attribute, a screen reader may miss entire sections of text.

To declare the language of your web page or HTML element, apply a **language attribute** on your HTML tags that declare the default language of the text in your web page. Doing so also enables the rest of the HTML elements on that page to inherit the same attributes.

Let's take a look at an example of how to handle incorporating a Spanish language declaration. Here is how it would look in HTML5 for Spanish:

```
<html lang="es">
```

Now that's a great start, but let's dig deeper on how to handle region sub-tags building on the same example of the Spanish language that is spoken across different countries and continents. According MDN Web Docs, es-ES is used for Spanish as spoken in Spain, but es-013 is Spanish as spoken in Central America. "International Spanish" would just be declared with es.[15]

Let's take a look at more examples to further illustrate:

```
<p lang="es-ES">This paragraph is defined as Spanish spoken in Spain.</p>
<p lang="es-013">This paragraph is defined as Spanish spoken in Central America.</p>

<p lang="es">This paragraph is defined as Spanish spoken internationally, with no specific region sub-tag defined.</p>
```

To learn more about the WCAG success criterion on language declaration, take a look at the following section: www.w3.org/TR/WCAG21/#language-of-page.

---

[15] https://developer.mozilla.org/en-US/docs/Web/HTML/Global_attributes/lang

Missing Transcript

Missing transcript impacts accessibility because there are many kinds of users that rely on closed captions to digest content. It's not just deaf, blind, or visually impaired users that require transcripts–you will also find that people on the neurodiverse spectrum deeply benefit from them!

Users with **cognitive disabilities or impairments** appreciate anything that helps them digest and understand new content in a way that won't overwhelm their sensitivities. This is because neurodiverse users often experience immense visual and/or auditory hypersensitivity. Closed captions and transcripts are tools that allow neurodiverse users to engage with content through an alternative means that won't overwhelm their senses. For example, if a neurodiverse user is overwhelmed by too much sound or the color contrast of a video, turning off the sound/video and studying from the transcript instead is a better alternative for digesting content more easily. For many users, transcripts are the only tool that empowers and supports them to fully follow along with your content.

To learn more, take a peek at what the **W3C Initiative** says about transcripts: `www.w3.org/WAI/media/av/transcripts/`.

Alternatively, if you also want to learn about the WCAG success criteria for transcripts, check out the following article: `www.w3.org/WAI/WCAG21/quickref/#audio-only-and-video-only-prerecorded`.

Moving Content (Slides/Carousel)

Moving content (such as a slideshow or carousel) impacts accessibility because there are several factors to consider for creating an inclusive slideshow. In reality, some argue that the benefit of moving content in slideshows and carousels is not significant enough to justify the sacrifice of accessibility.

To create an accessible carousel:[16]

- All functionality–including navigating–must be fully operable from a keyboard.

- Users should have the ability to pause your slideshow, in the event that the movement distracts them from processing the text content.

---

[16] `www.w3.org/WAI/tutorials/carousels/`

- Users should also be able to navigate and operate your slideshow via voice input software.

- All content must be fully labeled and described; don't forget to add alt-text for each image on your slideshow.

To learn more about the WCAG success criterion for this, check out the following two posts:

- www.w3.org/WAI/WCAG21/Understanding/pause-stop-hide.html

- www.w3.org/WAI/tutorials/carousels/

Justified Text

Justified Text impacts accessibility because it causes words to be either too close to each other or too far apart. Users with cognitive disabilities, such as dyslexia, may find it difficult to read and comprehend your content, which could potentially hinder their ability to fully engage with and understand the material. The best way to avoid this problem is to never apply fully justified text to your content layout.

To learn more about this, check out the following posts from W3C:

- www.w3.org/TR/WCAG20-TECHS/G169.html

- www.w3.org/TR/2008/REC-WCAG20-20081211/#visual-audio-contrast-visual-presentation

Small Font Sizes

Font Sizes across your site matter and also impact accessibility because they can cause strain to users with visibility impairments. And while WCAG doesn't mention any specific minimum font size requirements, they *do* mention that text should be able to be zoomed to 200% without pixelating.[17]

Remember to select a large enough font size (i.e., 12px or 16px) for web content, as this is still considered an important user experience consideration.

---

[17] www.w3.org/TR/UNDERSTANDING-WCAG20/visual-audio-contrast-scale.html

Free Screen Readers and Accessibility Testing Tools

Does your docs site pass the screen reader test?

Users who are blind or visually impaired rely on screen readers and assistive devices to be able to navigate the Web. Similar to sighted users, they too will "skim" content as they try to find information quickly. But the way that blind or visually impaired users are able to skim content is *different* and limited, because they're only able to skim web content on their screen reader.

The question arises: How do we ensure our Dev Docs website passes the many diverse accessibility success criteria? The only way to know for sure is to conduct testing via screen reader and accessibility testing tools.

Here are some great suggested tools to get started testing docs content:

- **Screen readers**: Literally grab an assistive device and attempt to navigate your docs web pages with It and take notes of what errors your encounter.

- **The AXE DevTools Web Accessibility Testing chrome extension**[18]

- **PowerMapper**: `http://try.powermapper.com/Demo/SortSite`

- **A11y Color Contrast validator**: `http://color.a11y.com/?wc3`

Extra Resources

Check out the **WAI** (Web Accessibility Initiative) *Accessibility Fundamentals* course: `www.w3.org/WAI/fundamentals/`.

In Closing

Before moving on to the next chapter, I encourage you to invest time furthering your understanding of accessibility. While this chapter covered some of the top accessibility issues and use cases, it is not an exhaustive guide. If you're ready to commit to

---

[18] `https://chrome.google.com/webstore/detail/axe-devtools-web-accessib/lhdoppojpmngadmnindnejefpokejbdd`

accessibility, the W3C Web Accessibility Initiative (WAI)[19] offers standards and support materials to help you implement accessibility best practices. You're not alone in this journey, as an entire community is dedicated to helping us improve in this area. Let's work toward a fully accessible future where all community members can confidently use your docs, regardless of any disability limitations they may have.

---

[19] www.w3.org/WAI/

CHAPTER 2

Information Architecture

In this chapter, I will dive into the engrossing world of Information Architecture (IA) as it relates to engineering documentation.

In this chapter, I aim to achieve three key goals. Firstly, I will provide insight into how to identify content buckets using the Diátaxis framework. Secondly, I will discuss the importance of defining user flows in your docs. Thirdly, I will explain the role of search functionality in IA. By the end of this chapter, you will have a comprehensive understanding of IA key concepts and be equipped with best practices to implement them in your own docs.

Why the Need?

Are you tired of wasting hours searching through engineering documentation only to come up empty-handed? Have you ever been frustrated by poorly structured documentation that makes it difficult to find the information you need? This is where Information Architecture (IA) comes in.

IA is crucial in docs because it provides a systematic approach to organizing information in a way that is meaningful and useful to the intended audience. Without proper IA, technical writers may create content that is confusing and difficult to navigate, leading to frustration and inefficiencies for community members. By identifying the top user flows and content buckets, you can design an IA that will make learning and debugging your development workflows easier.

Let's take a live example of what happens when content buckets and user flows are not clearly defined by referring to Figure 2-1. Imagine you're working on an AWS project and need to know how to stop an Amazon EC2 instance. You head over to AWS docs (`http://docs.aws.amazon.com`) and see a barrage of search results and left-hand navigation options, overwhelming you. It's not immediately clear which link you need, so you may end up clicking through several links before finding the right section.

A. Quetzalli, *Docs-as-Ecosystem*, https://doi.org/10.1007/978-1-4842-9328-7_2

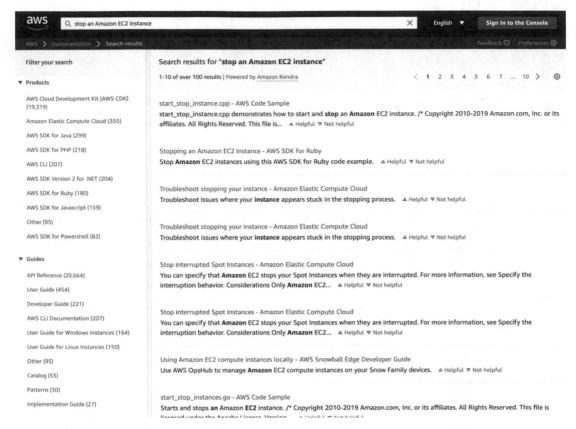

Figure 2-1. *AWS docs search results for the phrase "stop an Amazon EC2 instance"*

Now, imagine the improved user experience if we took time to identify core needs at a high level for diverse personas within your docs community. No matter which technology you work with, you need to learn how to set up your local development environment and try some basic tutorials. As you become more experienced, you'll encounter advanced use cases and troubleshooting scenarios. You may also appreciate a section that defines the main concepts or terms used by that technology.

Notice how we approached documentation content from an agnostic perspective in the previous paragraph without mentioning any specific technology or product. The agnostic content bucket approach revolutionizes docs IA.

Content Buckets

Content buckets refer to the logical grouping of information in a way that makes sense to community members. Organizing content into buckets is a critical aspect of IA because it allows community members to find the information they need quickly and efficiently. By grouping related information together, community members can navigate to the appropriate bucket and access the content they need without sifting through irrelevant or duplicate information. Effective content bucketing requires careful consideration of user needs and behaviors, as well as a deep understanding of the content road map.

Diátaxis Framework

The **Diátaxis framework**[1] provides a helpful classification system for organizing documentation content into four main agnostic content buckets: *tutorials, how-to guides, explanation*, and *reference*. (Refer to Figure 2-2.) These four categories provide a clear structure for organizing content in a way that is logical and easy to navigate for community members.

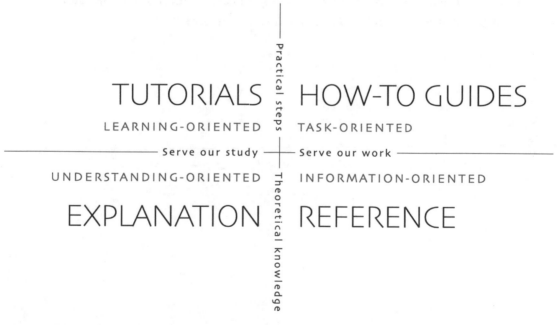

Figure 2-2. *The Diátaxis website (`https://Diátaxis.fr`) illustrates the four modes of documentation clearly and visually. The framework helps technical writers and engineers to identify the type of content they need to create for each bucket, making it easier for them to structure and organize documentation effectively*

---

[1] https://Diátaxis.fr

The first bucket, **tutorials**, is intended for community members who are new to a technology or product and need to learn basic processes or concepts by doing. Tutorials provide a step-by-step guide to accomplish a task or understand a concept.

The second bucket, **how-to guides**, addresses more complex or unique use cases that community members may encounter. These guides solve problems or provide advanced troubleshooting scenarios that a more active user would encounter.

The third bucket, **explanation**, is designed to define concepts within a technology's features and capabilities. This content provides a detailed explanation of concepts and terminology and is intended to help community members understand the technology they are working with more deeply.

The fourth and final bucket, **reference**, is intended for community members who need to access API specs and SDK docs. This content provides a detailed reference to the features and capabilities of a technology or product.

Figure 2-3 illustrates these four modes of technical documentation and their relationship with content buckets in the Diátaxis framework.

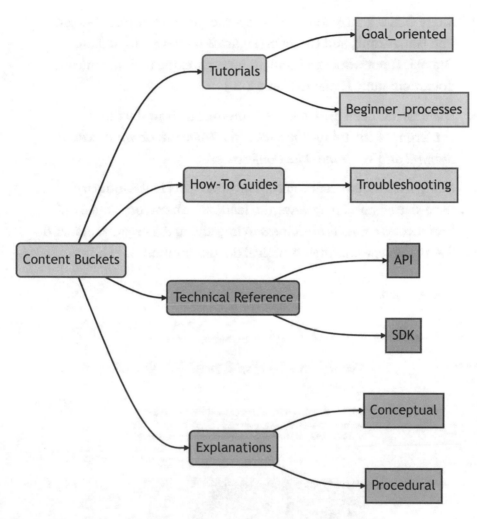

Figure 2-3. *The four modes of technical documentation and their relationship with content buckets in the Diátaxis framework, including tutorials, how-to guides, technical reference, and explanations, along with their subcategories*

Here are some reasons why the Diátaxis framework is well recognized in the technical writing field:

1. The Diátaxis framework is mentioned and recommended in various technical writing textbooks and resources, including *Developing Quality Technical Information* by Michelle Carey, Moira McFadden Lanyi, and Deirdre Longo and *Managing Enterprise Content: A Unified Content Strategy* by Ann Rockley and Charles Cooper.

2. Many OSS organizations and companies, including IBM, Google, Red Hat, Airbnb, and GatsbyJS (Figure 2-4), have adopted the Diátaxis framework as a standard for organizing their technical documentation. (Refer to Figure 2-3.)

3. Diátaxis has been presented at numerous technical writing conferences, including *The Society for Technical Communication Summit* and *Write the Docs Conferences.*

4. Many technical writers and content strategists in the industry have shared positive reviews and feedback about the Diátaxis framework, citing its usefulness in improving the organization and the effectiveness of their technical documentation.

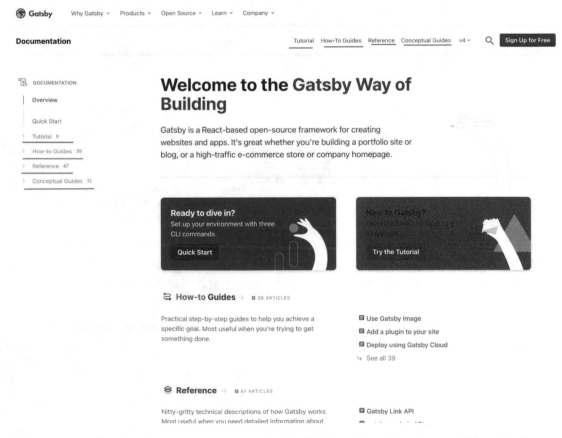

Figure 2-4. *Gatsby documentation website (*`http://gatsbyjs.com/docs`*) whose Information Architecture follows the Diátaxis four-part agnostic classification framework*

User Flows

Identifying user flows is a critical step in creating an effective IA for engineering documentation. User flows are the paths community members take to accomplish their goals when using a product or service. Figure 2-5 shows that identifying user flows in docs requires understanding the series of actions different personas take to find and use the information they need to complete a task.

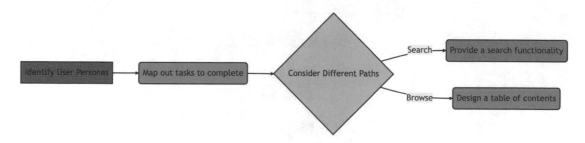

Figure 2-5. *Identifying user flows for Information Architecture in docs*

To identify user flows, you must first understand your community members and their needs. Start by identifying the different user personas that will be using your documentation. A user persona is a fictional representation of a group of community members with similar needs, goals, and characteristics.

Once you have identified your user personas, map out the tasks they will be trying to complete with your product or service. This will help you to identify the information they will need at each stage of the process.

Next, consider the different paths community members may take to complete these tasks. For example, a user may start by searching for a specific topic in your documentation, or they may start by browsing through the table of contents. By identifying the different paths community members may take, you can ensure that your Information Architecture is designed to accommodate all user needs.

Finally, consider the content buckets that will be most important to your community members. These are the categories of information that community members will need to access most frequently. By prioritizing these content buckets in your IA, you can ensure that community members can quickly and easily find the information they need.

Search Functionality

Search functionality is a critical component of IA in engineering documentation. It enables community members to quickly find the information they need without having to navigate through the entire document or sifting through irrelevant content. Figure 2-6 illustrates effective techniques for improved information retrieval in docs via search.

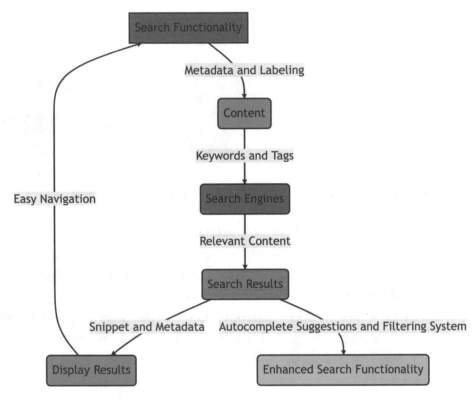

Figure 2-6. *Enhancing search functionality with metadata and filters*

Effective search functionality is achieved by implementing metadata and labeling for each piece of content in the documentation. This metadata includes keywords and tags that help search engines identify and retrieve the most relevant content for the user's query.

Additionally, search results should be presented in a way that is easy for community members to understand and navigate. This can be achieved by displaying a snippet of the content that matches the user's query, along with relevant metadata such as the title and author of the content.

Search functionality can also be enhanced by providing autocomplete suggestions and a filtering system that allows community members to narrow down their search results by specific criteria such as content buckets.

In Closing

Information Architecture is crucial for engineering documentation as it provides a framework for organizing and structuring information in a meaningful and usable way for the intended audience. To achieve effective IA, it's important to identify user flows, understand user search needs, and define clear content buckets. User flows change with time, which means you have to take your product road map into consideration so that you can better identify changes ahead in the road to your docs IA. Remember that IA is an ongoing process, not a one-time task.

My first recommendation is for you and your team to get started with the Diátaxis site and read their post on **"Understanding User Needs"**: `https://Diátaxis.fr/introduction`. As they mention in their site, "Diátaxis isn't just a framework for structuring documentation, it's a framework for understanding it, guiding the work of documentation authors, and assessing the quality of documentation."

My second recommendation is for you and your team to check out who else has adopted the **Diataxis framework**, which you can see on their site: `http://Diátaxis.fr/adoption`. By learning from their success stories and experiences, you can gain valuable insights into how to apply the framework to your own documentation.

Let's create an amazing future where any community member easily finds information in your docs!

CHAPTER 3

Search Engine Optimization

In this chapter, we will explore the relationship between search engine optimization (SEO) and engineering documentation sites. SEO is optimizing your website to make it easier for search engines to crawl ("read") and rank it in search results. By following search engine best practices, you can improve your docs' appearance in search results.

SEO is particularly important for engineering documentation because it improves the visibility of your content in Search Engine Results Pages (SERPs). Refer to Figure 3-1. As community members search for information related to your OSS technology or product, optimized documentation increases the likelihood that they will find and click on your content. Driving more traffic to your docs' website increases engagement with your product or OSS technology, making SEO critical to documentation success.

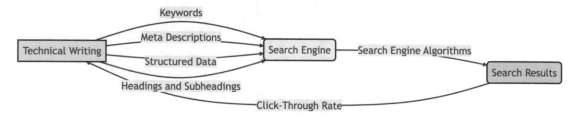

Figure 3-1. *The relationship between technical writing and SEO*

In this chapter, we will introduce both on-page and off-page SEO optimization techniques that you can use to improve your docs' visibility. We will also cover common SEO challenges and what the rise of Artificial Intelligence in SEO means for technical writers. By the end of the chapter, you will better understand SEO best practices and feel better equipped to optimize your engineering documentation for improved discoverability and accessibility.

A. Quetzalli, *Docs-as-Ecosystem*, https://doi.org/10.1007/978-1-4842-9328-7 3

Why the Need?

Monitoring SERPs is critical to the success of your docs' SEO strategy. Understanding the importance of SERPs and implementing effective SEO strategies increase your docs' visibility and accessibility. It is also important to regularly monitor your site's performance using analytics platforms (i.e., Google Analytics, Adobe Analytics, etc.) and third-party analytics tools (i.e., Matomo, Clicky, or Woopra), which provide valuable insights on your docs traffic and performance in search engines.

Search engines (i.e., Google, Bing, DuckDuckGo, etc.) and **web browsers** (i.e., Brave, Mozilla Firefox, Chrome, etc.) display search results differently for similar search phrases. As seen in Figures 3-2 to 3-5, searching for "node js docs" in various search engines and web browsers yields different results. Even small variations in search phrases, such as "nodejs documentation" (Figures 3-6 and 3-7), can yield unique search results. Regularly monitoring your documentation site's appearance in different search engines and web browsers for your target search phrases is vital to your project's success.

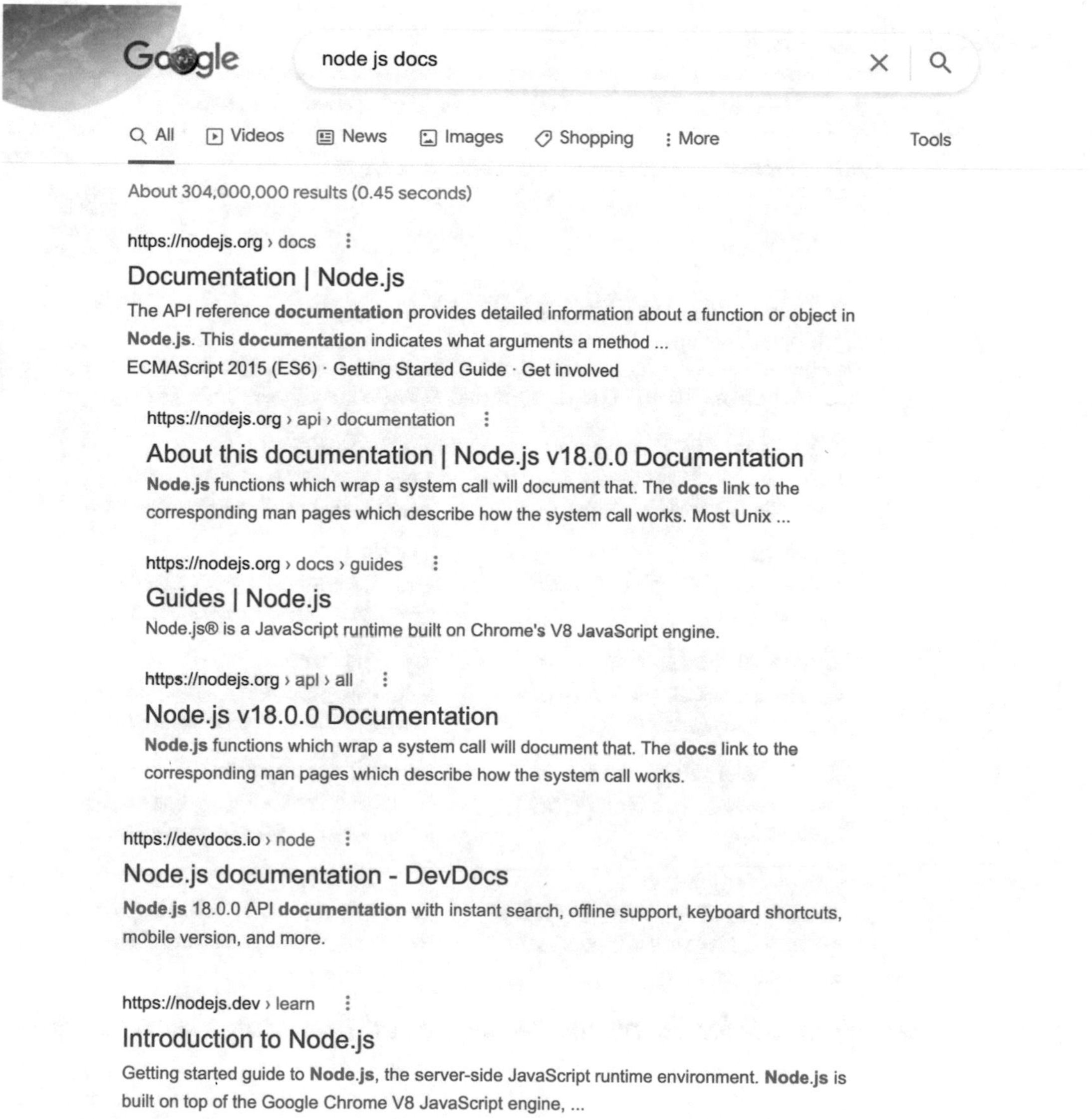

Google   node js docs   ✕ | 🔍

🔍 All   ▶ Videos   📰 News   🖼 Images   ◇ Shopping   ⋮ More   Tools

About 304,000,000 results (0.45 seconds)

https://nodejs.org › docs   ⋮
Documentation | Node.js
The API reference **documentation** provides detailed information about a function or object in
Node.js. This **documentation** indicates what arguments a method ...
ECMAScript 2015 (ES6) · Getting Started Guide · Get involved

https://nodejs.org › api › documentation   ⋮
About this documentation | Node.js v18.0.0 Documentation
Node.js functions which wrap a system call will document that. The **docs** link to the
corresponding man pages which describe how the system call works. Most Unix ...

https://nodejs.org › docs › guides   ⋮
Guides | Node.js
Node.js® is a JavaScript runtime built on Chrome's V8 JavaScript engine.

https://nodejs.org › apl › all   ⋮
Node.js v18.0.0 Documentation
Node.js functions which wrap a system call will document that. The **docs** link to the
corresponding man pages which describe how the system call works.

https://devdocs.io › node   ⋮
Node.js documentation - DevDocs
Node.js 18.0.0 API **documentation** with instant search, offline support, keyboard shortcuts,
mobile version, and more.

https://nodejs.dev › learn   ⋮
Introduction to Node.js
Getting started guide to **Node.js**, the server-side JavaScript runtime environment. **Node.js** is
built on top of the Google Chrome V8 JavaScript engine, ...

Figure 3-2. *Search results for the phrase "node js docs" from Google's
search engine*

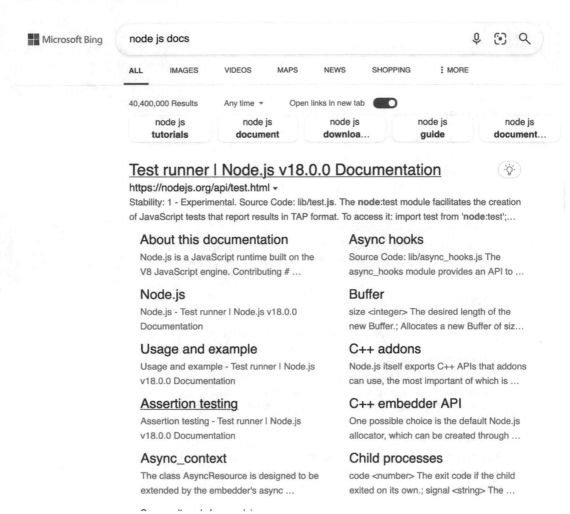

Figure 3-3. *Search results for the phrase "node js docs" from Bing's search engine*

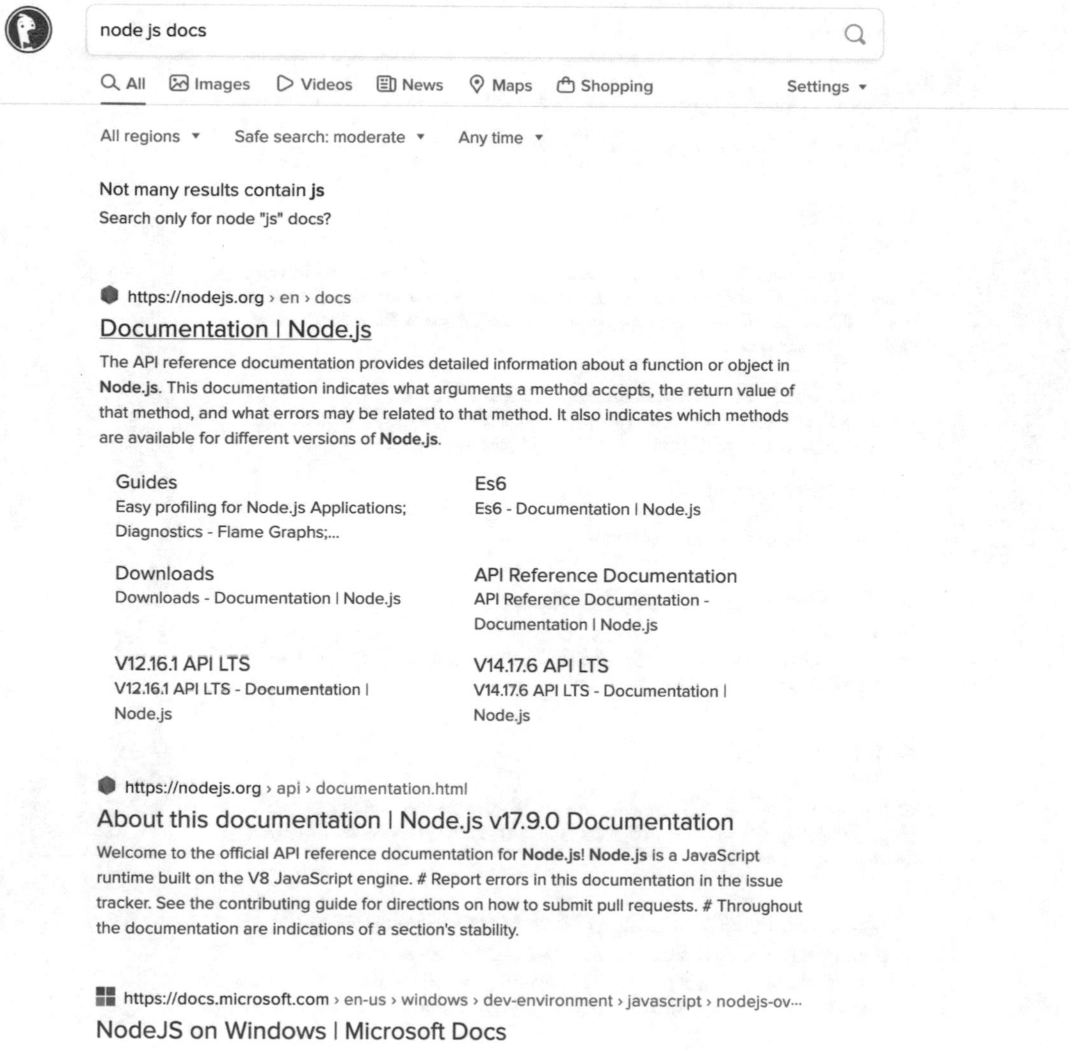

node js docs

Q All   🖼 Images   ▷ Videos   🗐 News   ⊙ Maps   🛍 Shopping   Settings ▾

All regions ▾   Safe search: moderate ▾   Any time ▾

Not many results contain **js**
Search only for node "js" docs?

⬤ https://nodejs.org › en › docs
Documentation | Node.js
The API reference documentation provides detailed information about a function or object in
Node.js. This documentation indicates what arguments a method accepts, the return value of
that method, and what errors may be related to that method. It also indicates which methods
are available for different versions of **Node.js**.

Guides	Es6
Easy profiling for Node.js Applications; Diagnostics - Flame Graphs;...	Es6 - Documentation	Node.js
Downloads	API Reference Documentation
Downloads - Documentation	Node.js	API Reference Documentation - Documentation	Node.js
V12.16.1 API LTS	V14.17.6 API LTS
V12.16.1 API LTS - Documentation	Node.js	V14.17.6 API LTS - Documentation	Node.js

⬤ https://nodejs.org › api › documentation.html
About this documentation | Node.js v17.9.0 Documentation
Welcome to the official API reference documentation for **Node.js**! **Node.js** is a JavaScript
runtime built on the V8 JavaScript engine. # Report errors in this documentation in the issue
tracker. See the contributing guide for directions on how to submit pull requests. # Throughout
the documentation are indications of a section's stability.

🔳 https://docs.microsoft.com › en-us › windows › dev-environment › javascript › nodejs-ov···
NodeJS on Windows | Microsoft Docs

Figure 3-4. *Search results for the phrase "node js docs" from the DuckDuckGo search engine*

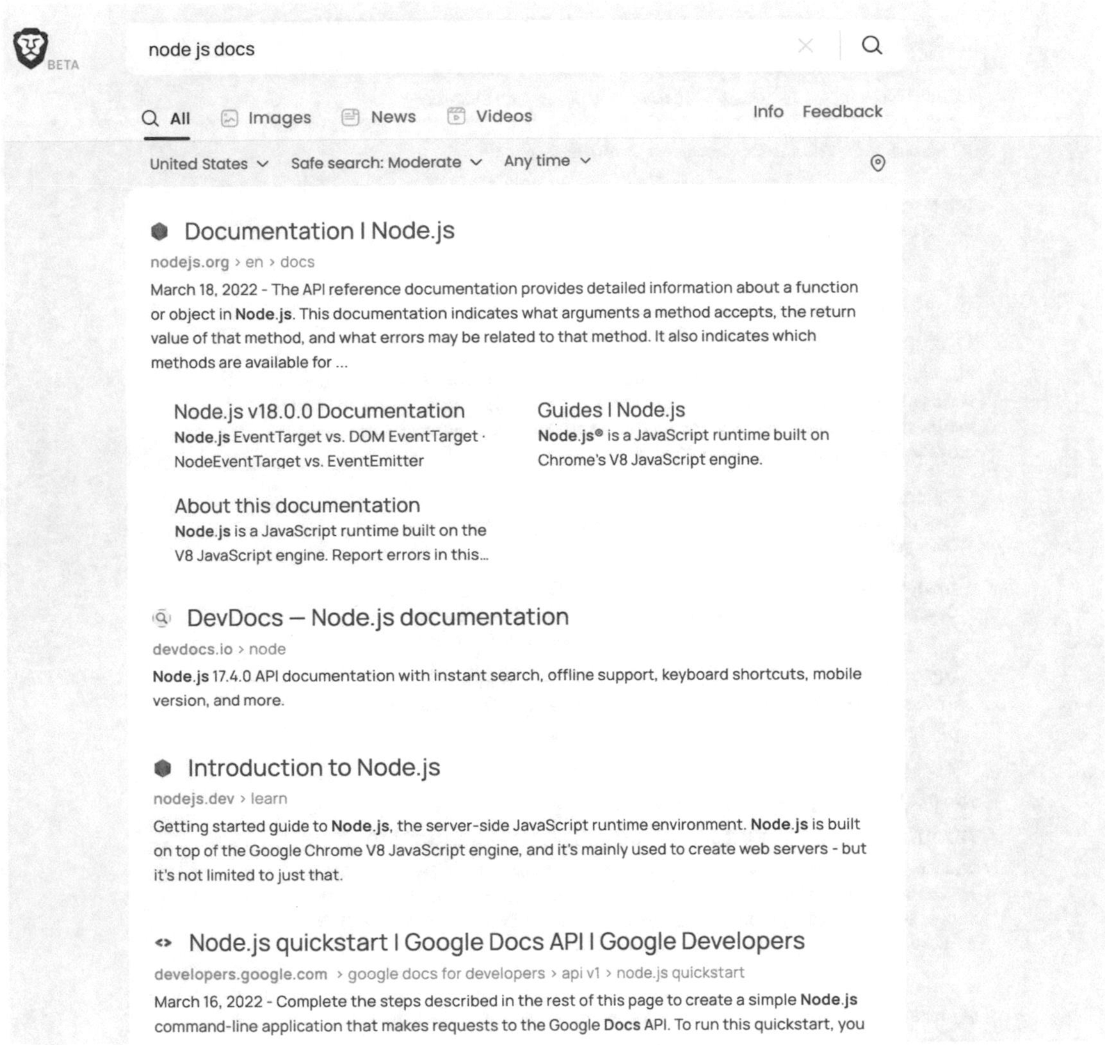

Figure 3-5. *Search results for the phrase "node js docs" from the web browser Brave*

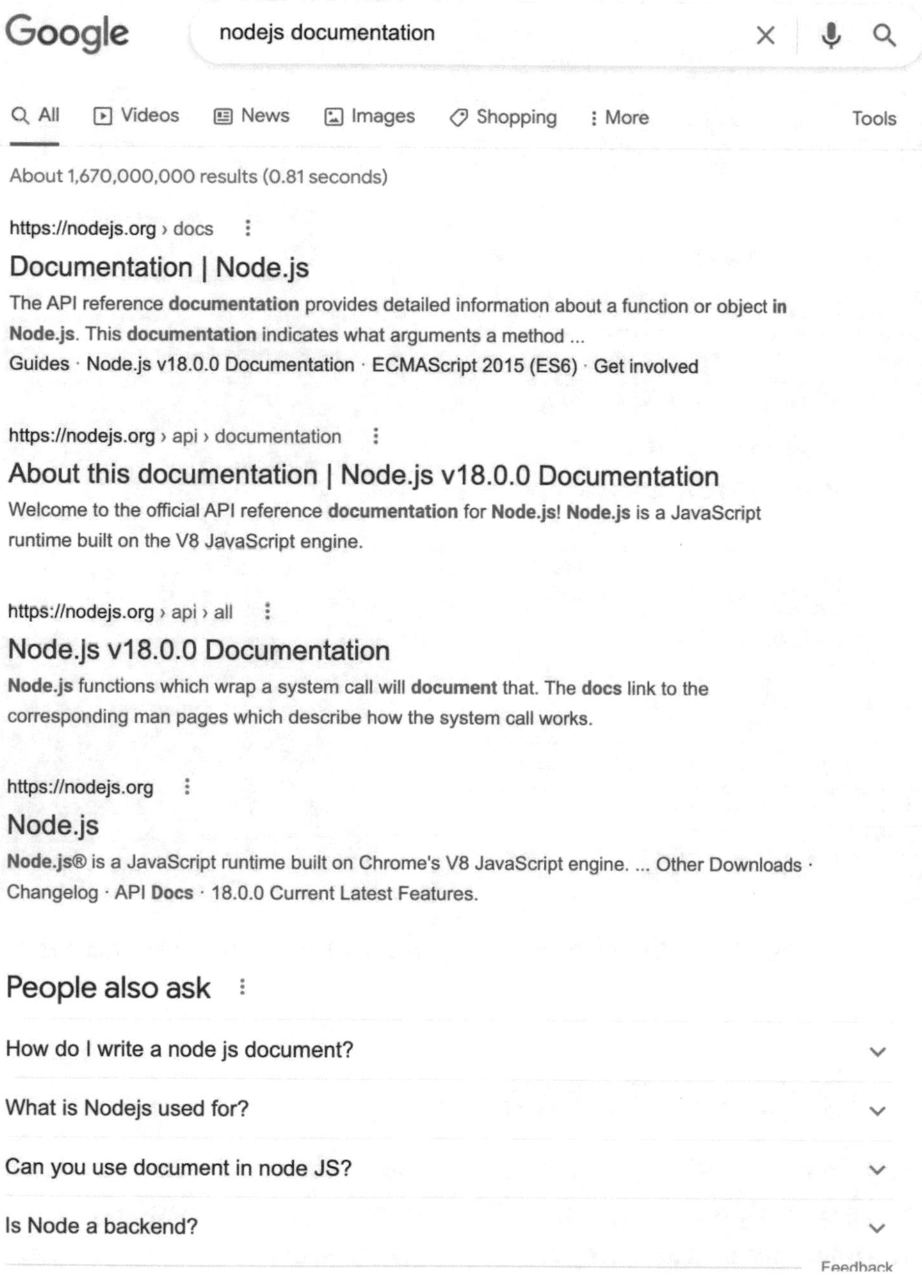

Google   nodejs documentation   ×   🎤   🔍

🔍 All   ▶ Videos   📰 News   🖼 Images   🔗 Shopping   ⋮ More   Tools

About 1,670,000,000 results (0.81 seconds)

https://nodejs.org › docs   ⋮
Documentation | Node.js
The API reference **documentation** provides detailed information about a function or object **in
Node.js**. This **documentation** indicates what arguments a method ...
Guides · Node.js v18.0.0 Documentation · ECMAScript 2015 (ES6) · Get involved

https://nodejs.org › api › documentation   ⋮
About this documentation | Node.js v18.0.0 Documentation
Welcome to the official API reference **documentation** for **Node.js**! **Node.js** is a JavaScript
runtime built on the V8 JavaScript engine.

https://nodejs.org › api › all   ⋮
Node.js v18.0.0 Documentation
Node.js functions which wrap a system call will **document** that. The **docs** link to the
corresponding man pages which describe how the system call works.

https://nodejs.org   ⋮
Node.js
Node.js® is a JavaScript runtime built on Chrome's V8 JavaScript engine. ... Other Downloads ·
Changelog · API **Docs** · 18.0.0 Current Latest Features.

People also ask   ⋮

How do I write a node js document?   ⌄

What is Nodejs used for?   ⌄

Can you use document in node JS?   ⌄

Is Node a backend?   ⌄
                                                                      Feedback

Figure 3-6. *Search results for the phrase "nodejs documentation" from Google's
search engine*

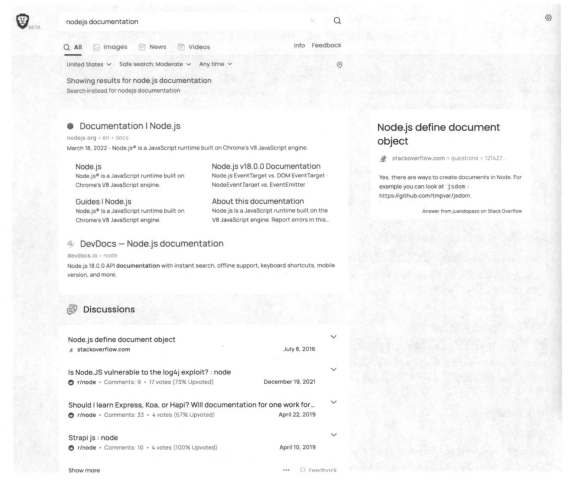

Figure 3-7. *Search results for the phrase "nodejs documentation" from the web browser Brave*

On-Page Optimization Techniques

On-page SEO optimization techniques focus on improving your docs website's content and HTML source code. By following best practices for on-page optimization, you can increase the relevance and authority of your content in search engines, ultimately leading to higher rankings in search results pages. This section will discuss various techniques such as keyword research and optimization, metadata optimization, content organization, navigation design, and URL structure. These techniques are essential for any technical writer who wants to make their documentation easily discoverable and accessible to their target audience.

Headers

Headers play an important role in SEO for engineering documentation by providing a hierarchical structure for your content, which helps search engines understand the main topics of your docs. Well-crafted headers improve your docs' readability and user experience. That said, it's important to include relevant keywords in your headers so that search engines understand your page's main topics and improve your rankings in search results. Remember to use keywords naturally and avoid keyword stuffing that harms rankings.

Many technical writers write their documentation using markup languages like HTML or Markdown. This allows them to easily add headers using specific tags, which search engines can interpret.

Here is an example of how headers can be coded using HTML:

```
<h1>Main Heading</h1>
<h2>Subheading content</h2>
<h3>More subheading content</h3>
```

In this example, the <h1> tag represents the main heading of the page, followed by <h2> and <h3> tags for subheadings. It is important to use headers in a logical and hierarchical order, as this helps both search engines and community members understand the structure of your content.

Here is an example of how headers can be marked up using Markdown, where the number of hash symbols before the text represents the header level:

```
# Introduction
## Background context
### Installation Guide
```

Page Titles and Meta Descriptions

Page titles and meta descriptions greatly impact the visibility of your engineering documentation in SERPs.

Page titles should be concise, descriptive, include targeted keywords, and be no longer than 60 characters to avoid being truncated in SERPs.

Here is an example of HTML syntax for a page title:

```
<head>
<title>Page Title - Targeted Keywords | OSS Project Name</title>
</head>
```

Meta descriptions summarize the page's content and greatly impact the click-through rate from SERPs. Meta descriptions should be no longer than 160 characters in length and should also include the targeted keywords.

Here is an example of HTML syntax for a meta description:

```
<head>
<title>Page Title - Target Keyword | Company Name</title>
<meta name="description" content="A summary of the page content, including targeted keywords.">
</head>
```

Keyword Research and Optimization

Keyword Research and Optimization involves identifying the specific words and phrases that community members will likely use when searching for information about your product or service and then incorporating those keywords strategically throughout your documentation site. Including relevant keywords in the page title, meta description, and content can help search engines understand what the page is about and improve its visibility in search results. It's also important to use keywords naturally and avoid "keyword stuffing," which is the practice of overusing keywords to manipulate search engine rankings.

Keyword research also involves analyzing search data and identifying the most relevant and high-volume keywords and phrases for which community members are searching. This research can be conducted using various tools, such as *Google Keyword Planner, SEMrush, Moz Keyword Explorer*, etc. By understanding the specific keywords and phrases that community members are searching for, you can optimize your documentation content to ensure it is relevant and easily discoverable.

While the meta keywords tag used to be an important factor in SEO, most search engines no longer consider it relevant. For example, Google has officially stated that it does not use the meta keywords tag as a ranking signal.[1]

---

[1] https://developers.google.com/search/blog/2009/09/google-does-not-use-keywords-meta-tag

In addition to traditional keyword research tools, Natural Language Processing and AI-powered tools can also be used to identify related keywords and phrases that can be used to optimize content for search engines. Ultimately, the goal of keyword research and optimization should be to improve the relevance and quality of content for both search engines and community members.

URL Structure

URL structure is how URLs are formatted and organized within your website's Information Architecture. A well-structured URL improves user experience, is easier to remember, and makes it easier for search engines to crawl when indexing your site.

Here are some best practices for URL structure:

1. **Keep URLs short and descriptive:** Use clear and concise words to describe the page's content. Avoid using numbers, symbols, or unnecessary words.

2. **Use hyphens to separate words:** Hyphens are preferred over underscores or spaces as they are more readable by humans and search engines.

3. **Include primary keywords:** Including primary keywords in the URL improves search engine rankings.

4. **Use lowercase letters:** URLs are case-sensitive, so it's best to use lowercase letters to avoid confusion.

5. **Ensure URL structure aligns with defined content buckets:** Including content buckets in your URL structure for your documentation site is crucial for creating a consistent and organized user experience and making it easier to navigate and find the information. Content buckets should inform your URL structure road map long term, helping you to plan and structure your URLs effectively.

To give you a starting point, here are some examples of URLs based on content buckets, such as *tutorials*, *how-to guides*, *explanations*, and *references:*

- **Tutorials:** domain.com/tutorials/title-of-tutorial

- **How-to guides:** domain.com/how-to/title-of-guide

- **Explanations:** domain.com/explanations/title-of-explanation

- **References:** domain.com/references/title-of-reference

Here are some well-structured URLs from GatsbyJS docs inspired by the content buckets recommended in the Diátaxis framework:

- **How-to guides:** `https://www.gatsbyjs.com/docs/how-to/routing/`

- **Explanations:** `https://www.gatsbyjs.com/docs/conceptual/overview-of-the-gatsby-build-process/`

- **Tutorials:** `https://www.gatsbyjs.com/docs/tutorial/getting-started/`

- **References:** `https://www.gatsbyjs.com/docs/reference/routing/file-system-route-api/`

Internal Linking

Internal linking refers to the practice of linking pages within the same website. Internal linking empowers community members to discover related content in your docs and helps search engines crawl and index your docs' site efficiently.

Here are a few best practices to keep in mind when implementing internal linking on your engineering documentation site:

1. **Use descriptive anchor text:** Anchor text is the clickable text that appears as a link. Use descriptive and accessible anchor text to help community members and search engines understand the linked page's content. For example, instead of using "click here" as your anchor text, use something more descriptive like "learn more about our Cool feature" or "check out the Cool feature troubleshooting guide."

2. **Link to relevant pages:** Internal links should be relevant and useful to community members.

3. **Don't overdo it:** While internal linking is important, it is also possible to overdo it. Too many internal links on a page appear spammy and hurt the user experience.

Here is an example of internal linking using HTML:

```
<p>Read our <a href="/cool-feature">Cool feature docs</a> for more
information.</p>
```

Here is that same internal linking example using Markup:

```
Read our [Cool feature docs](#cool-feature) for more information.
```

Image Optimization

Image optimization involves optimizing the images on your site so that they are easily discoverable and understandable by search engine crawlers. The three main areas to focus on are *alt tags*, *file names*, and *image size*.

Alt tags should provide descriptive text explaining the image's content and purpose. This helps screen readers and search engines understand the image context and improve accessibility for community members with visual impairments.

Here's an example of how to add an alt tag using markup syntax:

```
![alt text](path/to/image.jpg "Optional title")
```

File names should also be descriptive and include relevant keywords if possible. Avoid using generic file names like "image1.jpg" or "photo.png". Instead, use a file name that accurately describes the image, such as "green-notebook-product.jpg". Using hyphens instead of underscores or spaces in file names helps with file name readability for both humans and search engine crawlers.

Image size is also important for optimization. Large image files slow down page loading times, negatively impacting your site's ranking in search results. Resizing and compressing images reduce file size without sacrificing image quality. Optimizing image sizes before uploading them to a website or application is better than relying on CSS or JS to resize them because that can slow down page load times, negatively impacting SEO and user experience. However, there may be cases where resizing images using CSS or JS is appropriate, such as when serving different sizes of the same image for different devices.

Navigation

The navigation menu items of your docs' site help search engines understand your main content hierarchy and which pages/sections you deem the most important. Search engines can crawl your site more efficiently when your navigation highlights the most important sections and content.

Figure 3-8 outlines navigation menu items from the OSS initiative, AsyncAPI, demonstrating a clear hierarchy of important sections.

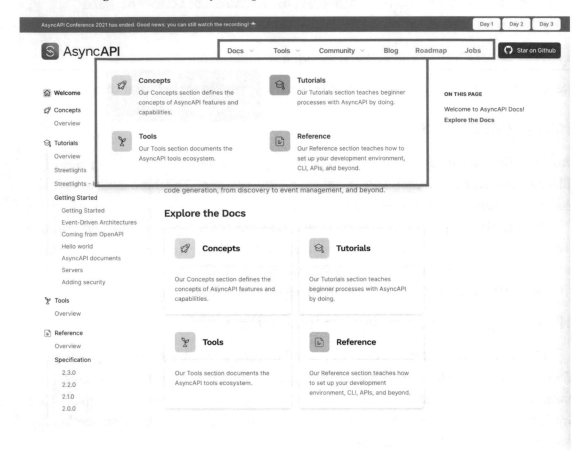

Figure 3-8. *Navigation menu items from the OSS initiative, AsyncAPI*

But the main menu navigation isn't the only navigation on a docs site! Most docs sites have both left-hand and right-hand navigation items. But regardless of which navigation you have, they all affect search engine results.

Let's look at an example from Django docs navigation items and Django search results that display the same items found on the Django website. (You'll even see a hyperlink shown in the search results.)

Figure 3-9 outlines right-hand navigation menu items from the OSS initiative, Django, and how they appear in search results. (These search results are from the search engine Google.)

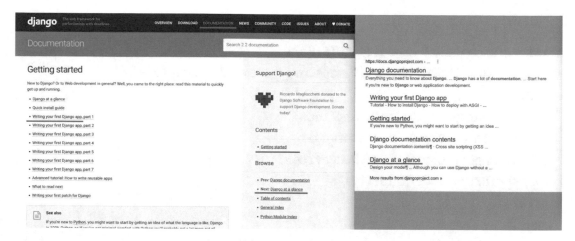

Figure 3-9.   *This image outlines right-hand navigation menu items from the OSS initiative, Django, and how they appear in search results. (These search results are from the search engine Google)*

Page Loading Time

Page loading time is a critical factor in SEO. The longer it takes for your docs website pages to load, the higher the chances of frustrating your community members, causing them to leave your site. Search engines track the percentage of community members that bounce out of your website early and how long it takes for each page to load. A clunky docs site that doesn't load efficiently quickly leads to search engine penalties and poor user experience.

Monitor your docs page loading times in your analytics platform(s) of choice, tracking different page loading times across your docs' site. You can also implement various optimization techniques, such as compressing images, enabling caching, and minimizing HTTP requests to improve the page loading time of your site.

Sitemaps

In the context of on-page optimization, a sitemap is a file that lists a website's important pages organized hierarchically. Including a sitemap on your documentation site improves the visibility and search ranking of your content by providing search engines with a clear and organized view of your site's content structure. Sitemaps can be updated manually or with automated content management systems and plug-ins.

Here is a sitemap example:

```xml
<?xml version="1.0" encoding="UTF-8"?>
<urlset xmlns="http://www.sitemaps.org/schemas/sitemap/0.9">
   <url>
      <loc>http://example.com/</loc>
      <lastmod>2023-05-10</lastmod>
      <changefreq>monthly</changefreq>
      <priority>1.0</priority>
   </url>
   <url>
      <loc>http://example.com/page1.html</loc>
      <lastmod>2023-05-09</lastmod>
      <changefreq>weekly</changefreq>
      <priority>0.8</priority>
   </url>
   <url>
      <loc>http://example.com/page2.html</loc>
      <lastmod>2023-05-08</lastmod>
      <changefreq>weekly</changefreq>
      <priority>0.8</priority>
   </url>
</urlset>
```

In this example, the sitemap lists three URLs from a hypothetical website. Each URL includes the <loc> element for the location URL of the page, <lastmod> for the last modified date, <changefreq> for the expected frequency of changes on the page, and <priority> to indicate the relative importance of the page compared to others on the site.

Here are some on-page optimization techniques specific to sitemaps for docs:

1. **Include all important pages:** Ensure that your sitemap includes all important pages of your docs' website. Include all pages you want search engines to index, such as main category pages, individual documentation pages, and any other important pages.

2. **Prioritize pages:** Prioritize the important pages in your sitemap by placing them at the top of the file. You can use the <priority> tag in your sitemap. This tag allows you to specify the priority of each page, with a value between 0.0 and 1.0, with 1.0 being the highest priority.

3. **Use last modification dates:** Include the last modification date for each page in your sitemap to help search engines understand the update frequency for your pages and prioritize crawling the more frequently updated pages.

4. **Consider image and video sitemaps:** If your docs' website includes images or videos, consider creating separate sitemaps for them. Helping search engines better understand your docs' content improves your visibility in SERPs.

Off-Page Optimization Techniques

Off-page SEO optimization techniques focus on improving factors outside your docs' website, such as backlinks and social media presence. These factors can significantly impact the visibility and authority of your website in Search Engine Results Pages (SERPs). This section will explore various off-page optimization techniques to improve your docs' search engine rankings and overall online presence.

Backlinking

Backlinking is an essential off-page SEO optimization technique that involves acquiring links from other websites that point to your website. These links are also known as inbound links or incoming links. The number and quality of backlinks to your docs' website are crucial factors in determining your search engine ranking. The more high-quality backlinks your docs' website has, the more likely it is to rank higher in SERPs. Backlinking is an effective way to increase your website's visibility, credibility, and authority.

Robots.txt File

The robots.txt file is critical in managing search engine crawlers' interaction with your docs' website. It guides the crawlers, telling them which URLs they can access and crawl on your site. Properly configuring this file can help prevent your site from becoming overloaded with unnecessary crawler traffic.

Here's an example of the format for a robots.txt file, which includes instructions for specific user agents, directives for allowing and disallowing certain URLs, and exclusion strings for URLs that should not be crawled:

```
User-agent: [user-agent name]
Allow: /my-best-content-ever/
Disallow: /practice-subfolder/
[URL string not to be crawled]
```

Crawling and Indexing

Crawling and indexing are two essential components of SEO. Crawling refers to search engines finding and analyzing various types of content on your docs' website, such as images, videos, PDFs, and social media posts. Search engines continually crawl your site for new and updated content, making it crucial to ensure that all pages are accessible for crawling.

Indexing involves adding web pages to the search engine's database to appear in search results. After crawling your site, search engines determine which pages to index and analyze them for relevance and importance. Optimizing your site for indexing can improve your search engine ranking and increase the visibility of your target audience.

Sitemaps

In the context of off-page optimization, sitemaps help search engines better understand the structure of a website and its content, allowing them to crawl more effectively and index pages.

One off-page optimization technique for sitemaps is to submit them to search engines through their webmaster tools or APIs. This allows search engines to regularly crawl the website and ensure that any new or updated pages are included in the sitemap. Another technique is to submit the sitemap to online directories and search engines beyond just Google, such as Bing and Yahoo, increasing your docs' visibility and accessibility for a wider audience.

Online Forums and Social Media

Online forums and social media platforms play a crucial role in off-page SEO optimization for your docs' site. These platforms provide an opportunity to engage with your community members, answer their questions, and provide them with valuable information they may be unable to find on your docs. Doing so establishes expertise in your field and builds a relationship with your community.

One important aspect of leveraging online forums and social media for SEO is to include links to your documentation site in your posts and responses. This can help drive traffic to your site and increase its visibility. However, it's important to note that simply spamming links to your site without providing any value or engaging with your audience is not an effective strategy and may even result in penalties from search engines.

In addition to including links to your documentation site, you should frequently optimize your social media and forum profiles to improve your visibility in search results. Use relevant keywords in your profile description and posts, and include links to your docs in your profile.

Common SEO Challenges

While optimizing your documentation site for search engines can lead to significant benefits, it also comes with challenges. One of the main challenges is ensuring that your site does not contain duplicate content, which can harm your search engine rankings. This section will discuss the importance of implementing internationalization best practices and using canonical tags to help search engines understand which pages should be prioritized for indexing.

Duplicate Content and Canonical Pages

Duplicate content is a major SEO issue because search engines prefer unique and original content. Duplicate content appears on multiple pages, whether on your docs' website or other platforms where your content has been copied and cross-posted.

One way to avoid the negative impact of duplicate content is through the use of canonical tags. Adding a canonical tag to all of your duplicate pages indicates to search engines which page is the "main" (canonical) page and prevents duplicate pages from being flagged as duplicate content.

Here's a canonical tag example in HTML:

```
<!DOCTYPE html>
<html>
  <head>
    <title>Docs</title>
    <link rel="canonical" href="https://www.messagedriven.com/docs/
    explanation/message-driven-architecture">
  </head>
  <body>
    <h1>Welcome to Message Driven Docs!</h1>
  </body>
</html>
```

In the preceding code, the link element with the rel attribute set to canonical indicates to search engines that the page at the specified URL (`https://www.messagedriven.com/docs/explanation/message-driven-architecture`) is the preferred (canonical) version of this content, even if there are other duplicate versions of the page content available at different URLs.

Internationalization (i18n)

Internationalization (i18n) is a crucial part of SEO that involves optimizing your website for search engines to identify the countries and languages you are targeting. In HTML, you can specify the target language and country using the "lang" attribute in the "html" tag. Let's take a look at some examples.

Targeting English for language and Canada for country:

```
<!DOCTYPE html>
<html lang="en-ca">
```

Targeting Spanish for language and Mexico for country:

```
<!DOCTYPE html>
<html lang="es-mx">
```

Targeting Spanish for language and Spain for country:

```
<!DOCTYPE html>
<html lang="es-es">
```

Targeting German for language and Germany for country:

```
<!DOCTYPE html>
<html lang="de-DE">
```

And for a bit of fun, here's an example targeting Swedish for language and Sweden for country:

```
<!DOCTYPE html>
<html lang="sv-SE">
```

The Rise of Artificial Intelligence in SEO

With the rise of Artificial Intelligence (AI) in SEO, the way people interact with search engines has changed. AI has shifted the focus from short, keyword-based queries to conversational language queries. In this section, we will explore how AI is transforming the field of SEO and what it means for optimizing your documentation website.

Machine Learning in Search Algorithms

Machine learning (ML) is a type of AI revolutionizing the way search algorithms work. ML algorithms analyze large amounts of data and learn from it, without being explicitly programmed. In the context of search algorithms, ML helps search engines better understand user search intent and context, leading to more accurate search results. In fact, ML is even used to detect and penalize black hat SEO techniques, such as keyword stuffing and link schemes.

ML algorithms also analyze user behavior data to determine which pages are most relevant to certain search queries and adjust search rankings accordingly. For example, if users consistently click on a particular page for a specific search query, the ML algorithm may give that page a higher ranking for that query in the future.

Natural Language Processing, Voice Search, and Chatbots

Natural Language Processing (NLP) is another subfield of AI focusing on enabling machines to understand and interpret human language. In SEO, NLP helps search engines understand the context of search queries and content on web pages. NLP has led to the rise of voice search and chatbots, which relies heavily on NLP to provide accurate and relevant results in conversational query format.

Voice search is a rapidly growing trend in SEO, as numerous users are used to searching for information using voice assistants such as Siri, Alexa, and Google Assistant. Optimizing content for voice search requires a focus on long-tail keywords and conversational language. It's also important to consider the different devices and platforms that users may be using to perform voice searches.

Chatbots (i.e., ChatGPT) are another application of NLP in SEO. Chatbots are used to engage with users and provide them with relevant information or assistance. Optimizing chatbots for SEO requires a focus on providing relevant and helpful responses to users, as well as incorporating relevant keywords and topics into the chatbot's responses.

Here are some examples of how technical writers can leverage ChatGPT for their docs' SEO strategy:

- **Researching keywords:** ChatGPT can be used to generate a list of keywords related to your topic.

- **Generating content ideas:** If you're struggling to come up with new ideas for content, ChatGPT can suggest documentation topics based on your existing docs content and industry trends.

- **Checking content quality:** ChatGPT can check the readability and coherence of your content, which can impact your search engine ranking.

- **Writing meta descriptions:** ChatGPT can generate concise and compelling meta descriptions for your pages to increase click-through rates from SERPs.

AI Search Engines

AI search engines are transforming the way people search for information online. These search engines are designed to understand natural language queries and provide relevant search results based on the user's intent. They use ML algorithms to analyze vast amounts of data, learn from user behavior, and continuously improve the accuracy of search results.

One example of an AI search engine is Phind,[2] specifically designed for programming topics. Phind understands technical queries, code snippets, and programming languages. Phind generates a detailed answer using its AI algorithms and shows links to web search results, providing a quick and efficient way for technical writers to find information. As seen in Figures 3-10 and 3-11, Phind can generate detailed answers to queries such as "help me write an AsyncAPI yaml document" and "help me write a docker image."

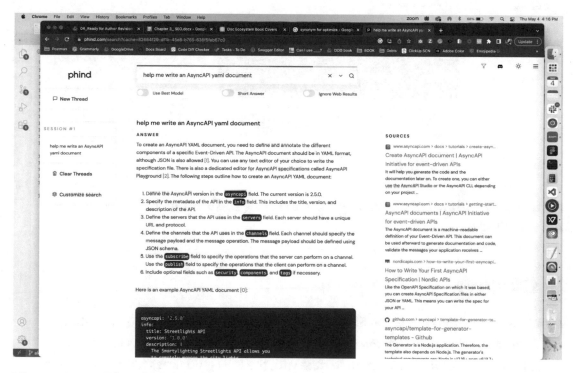

Figure 3-10. *Phind AI search engine generating answer for "help me write an AsyncAPI yaml document"*

[2] www.phind.com/

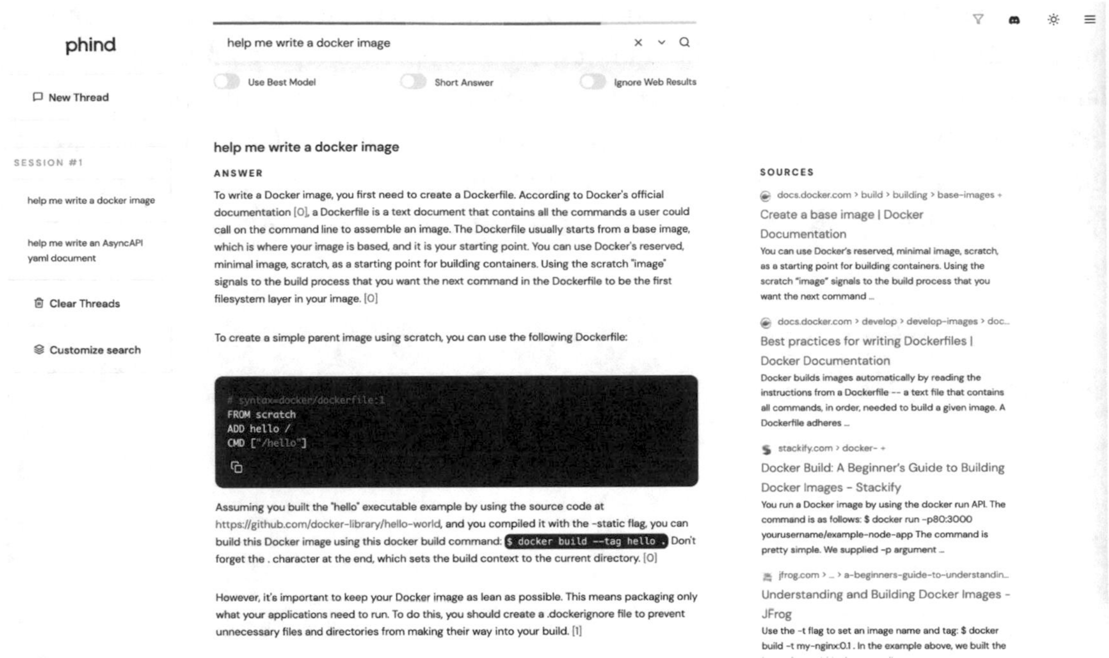

Figure 3-11. *Phind AI search engine generating answer for "help me write a docker image"*

In Closing

As we conclude this chapter on SEO for docs, remember to invest time in reading the documentation of the search engines you rely on the most, such as Google and Bing. It's also important to keep up to date with the SEO guidelines for other popular search engines, such as DuckDuckGo or Baidu, especially for international community members.

In addition to search engines, remember to also focus on optimizing docs content for voice search and chatbots. With the rise of AI in SEO, it's important to stay up to date with the latest technology and tools, such as Phind, an AI-powered search engine.

Now that you have a solid understanding of SEO for docs, it's time to move forward to the next chapter and focus on improving the User Experience (UX) of your documentation site.

CHAPTER 4

User Interface and User Experience

In this chapter, we will delve into the worlds of User Interface (UI) and User Experience (UX) as they apply to designing documentation sites. We will cover the essential design components necessary to provide an optimal UX/UI for all community members, including search, responsive design, mobile menu items, font size, color accessibility considerations, and a dedicated documentation home page. By the end of this chapter, you will have a better understanding of how to communicate with designers, how to maintain close collaboration, and how to receive and accept feedback. Remember, the key to a successful relationship with your designer is trust!

Why the Need?

Have you ever scrunched your nose or squinted in frustration while navigating through documentation? If so, you're not alone. This experience can be attributed to a lack of investment in the design budget, which unfortunately happens far too often in docs. While it may seem like a small detail, the truth is that a well-designed documentation site makes all the difference in the world to user experience.

By learning from the mistakes of past bad experiences, we can invest in doing things right and moving forward. When navigating documentation, community members should be able to interact and find information seamlessly, regardless of their device. The better the design, the better the learning experience for everyone involved. Let's allocate enough resources for design in our documentation projects and make our docs a delightful educational experience for the entire community.

© Alejandra Quetzalli 2023
A. Quetzalli, *Docs-as-Ecosystem*, https://doi.org/10.1007/978-1-4842-9328-7_4

Collaboration with Designers

Collaboration between designers and technical writers is crucial for the success of a docs project, as shown in Figure 4-1. Establish clear goals and objectives, frequently sharing perspectives and knowledge. Building trust among community members is also critical for aligning design and docs contributions. Trust facilitates direct feedback and easier collaboration every step of the way. Regular syncs between designers, product managers, engineering leads, and diverse community member stakeholders can resolve pending docs design questions and ensure cross-functional collaborations with technical writers.

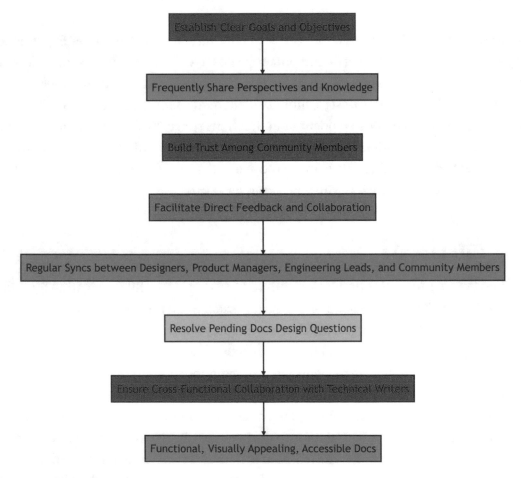

Figure 4-1. *Collaboration between designers and technical writers is crucial for the success of a docs project*

It is crucial to emphasize the involvement of designers in documentation work and processes. Unfortunately, some organizations dismiss the need for design contributions for their documentation, which is a significant oversight since documentation must be a collaborative community effort involving diverse stakeholders. Designer collaboration brings a fresh perspective to the documentation, ensuring the content is functional, visually appealing, and accessible.

Docs Home Page

A dedicated home page outlining the content buckets in your documentation is a centralized hub for community members to navigate information. Providing clear learning paths and highlighting content buckets help community members quickly identify the needed information, leading to better retention and engagement.

One great example of a dedicated docs home page is the one on GatsbyJS's website, as seen in Figure 4-2. The home page welcomes readers with an introduction header and paragraph overviewing the technology. The content buckets are also clearly outlined and highlighted, making it easy for users to find the necessary information.

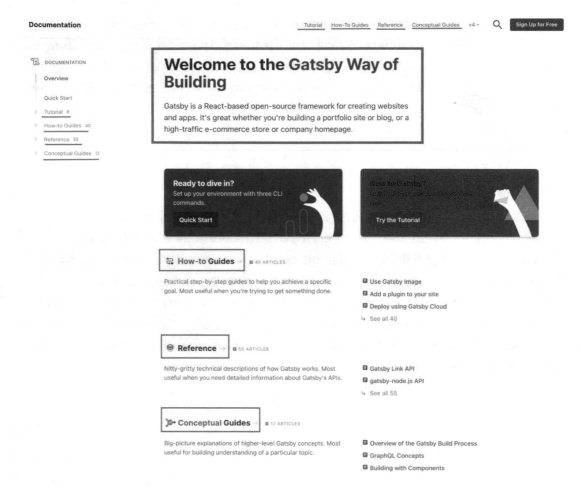

Figure 4-2. *The GatsbyJS docs home page showing dedicated content buckets*

AsyncAPI's dedicated docs home page is also a great example, seen in Figure 4-3, using cards to highlight the content buckets and welcome community members with an introduction paragraph.

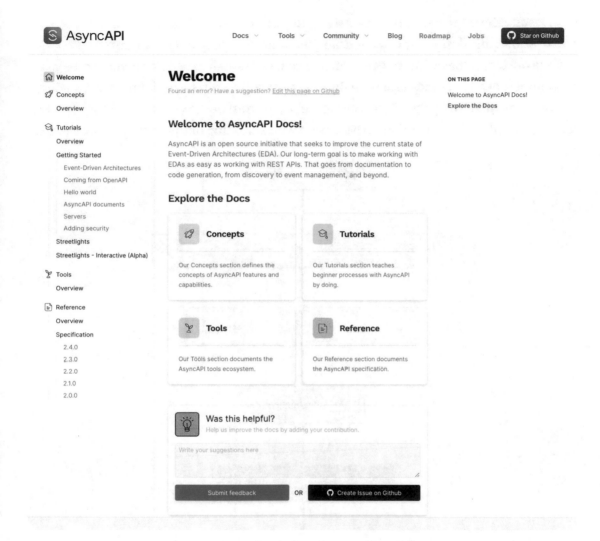

Figure 4-3. *The AsyncAPI docs home page showing dedicated content buckets*

Responsive Design

Responsive design is critical to ensure your docs can be accessed and used seamlessly across various devices, including mobile phones and tablets. Some best practices for responsive design in docs include using a mobile-first approach, designing for touchscreens, optimizing images for different screen sizes, and using a flexible grid system, as discussed in Figure 4-4.

Despite the importance of responsive design, many docs sites and sections still overlook this design aspect. For example, some sites may not be optimized for mobile devices or have font sizes and menu items too small to use on smaller screens. Sometimes, designers may intentionally not optimize certain pages for mobile viewing, assuming readers will primarily access those pages from desktops. To avoid such issues, it is important to prioritize responsive design when creating or updating your docs' site.

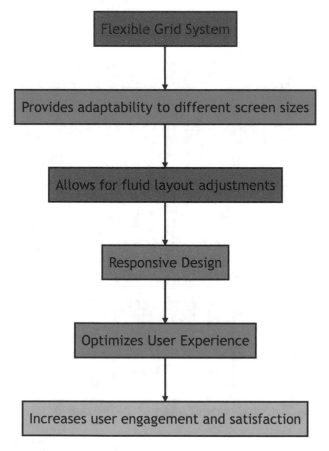

Figure 4-4. *Incorporating responsive design in your documentation*

Figure 4-5 shows an example of a Checkout Quickstart from Stripe's DevDocs that was not designed to be mobile responsive, while Figure 4-6 shows an example of a Reddit docs site not responsive at all.

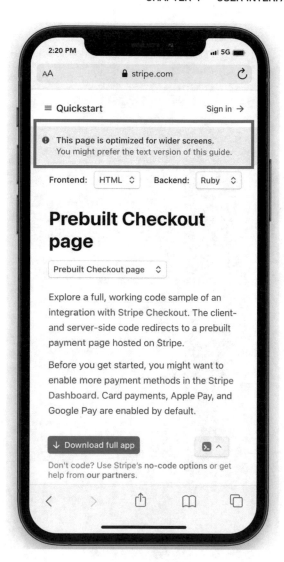

Figure 4-5. *A Checkout Quickstart example from Stripe's docs that isn't mobile optimized*

Figure 4-6.   *The Reddit API docs[1] site isn't mobile responsive*

---

[1] www.reddit.com/dev/api/

Colors

When designing documentation, colors are important in creating a visually appealing and easy-to-read website. However, color choices also significantly impact accessibility for all community members, including those with visual impairments. Chapter 1 discussed the importance of color contrast in accessibility, which applies to selecting your docs' site's primary and secondary colors.

The Web Content Accessibility Guidelines (WCAG) provides a standard of at least 4.5:1 for text and interactive elements' color contrast ratio to ensure viewers with visual impairments can read the text. This ratio is calculated by dividing the luminance of the lighter color by the darker color. For people with visual impairments or who use low-light or high-glare conditions, a 4.5:1 ratio is essential for legibility.

The Carnegie Museum website offers color palette combination examples that fall within the ranges of WCAG compliance, as shown in Figure 4-7 for colors on a white background and Figure 4-8 for neutrals on a colored background.

Colors on a white background

#112e51 on #ffffff	#205493 on #ffffff
#0071bc on #ffffff	#205493 on #ffffff
#046b99 on #ffffff	#2e8540 on #ffffff
#4c2c92 on #ffffff	#212121 on #ffffff
#323a45 on #ffffff	#5b616b on #ffffff
#494440 on #ffffff	#981b1e on #ffffff
#cd2026 on #ffffff	#e31c3d on #ffffff

Figure 4-7. *"Colors on a white background," referenced from CarnegieMuseum.org*

Neutrals on a colored background

Figure 4-8. *"Neutrals on a colored background," referenced from CarnegieMuseum.org*

One way to ensure that the colors used in your docs meet WCAG guidelines is to use a color contrast checker tool such as the **WebAIM Color Contrast Checker**.[2] These tools allow you to input the color values for your text and background and provide a contrast ratio score to determine if it meets WCAG guidelines. If the score meets or exceeds the minimum requirement of 4.5:1, the colors have sufficient contrast.

Typography

Typography is another critical aspect of designing docs for an excellent user experience. Font selection and sizing significantly affect readability, especially on mobile devices. The font size and style should be consistent throughout the site, ensuring the community member does not get lost while navigating between pages.

Regarding typography, it is essential to consider the difference between desktop and mobile devices. Desktop devices tend to have larger screens and higher resolutions, meaning text can be smaller and still be legible. However, on mobile devices, the screen is smaller, and the text can be difficult to read if the font size is too small. Therefore, choosing a font size that is easy to read on both desktop and mobile devices is crucial.

For desktop devices, a general guideline is to use a font size of at least 16 pixels for body text and a larger size for headings and subheadings. It's important also to consider line spacing, as text that is too tightly spaced can be difficult to read.

For mobile devices, a font size of at least 14 pixels for body text and a larger size for headings and subheadings are recommended. Mobile devices have smaller screens, so it's important to ensure that text is legible without zooming in.

Figure 4-9 shows an example from Kotlin docs[3] of font sizing on mobile. The paragraph font size is a good example of a legible size on mobile screens.

---

[2] https://webaim.org/resources/contrastchecker/
[3] https://kotlinlang.org/docs

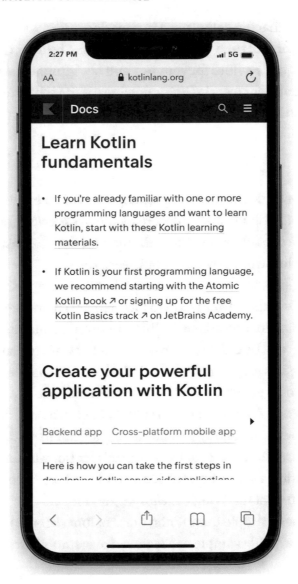

Figure 4-9. *Kotlin docs example of mobile font sizing*

Figure 4-10 shows a similar example from AsyncAPI Docs,[4] where the chosen fonts and spacing create a pleasant reading experience.

---

[4]`https://asyncapi.com/docs`

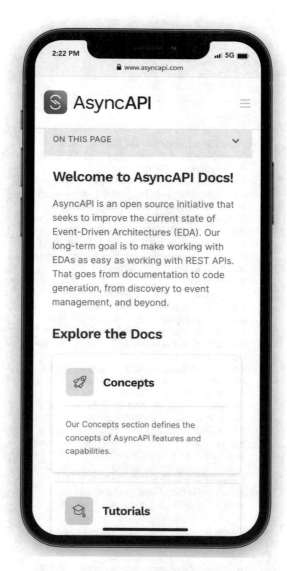

Figure 4-10. *AsyncAPI Docs example of mobile font sizing*

Figure 4-11 is an example from the Python 3 Installation docs[5] that highlights the importance of adequate whitespace around smaller fonts on mobile. Without enough spacing, text can become difficult to read and understand.

---

[5] https://docs.python.org/3/using/index.html

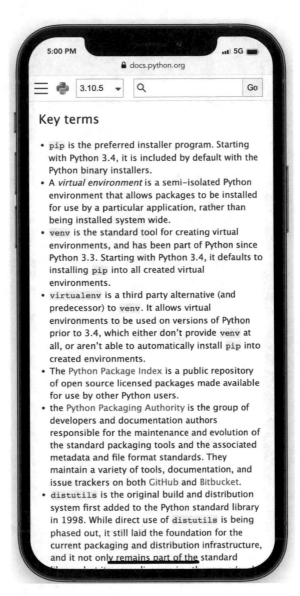

Figure 4-11. *Python 3 docs example of mobile font sizing and spacing*

When designing font size and spacing for docs, prioritize readability and ensure content is accessible to all community members. Following these best practices allows readers to find and comprehend docs information easily.

Navigation

In documentation sites, carefully designed navigation elements should align with designated content buckets to ensure community members can identify their learning path. In the mobile realm, paying particular attention to menu item sizing, font size, and spacing is essential. The menu items and icons should be large enough for community members with different finger sizes to navigate. Your menu items should be logically highlighted and correlate with your chosen content buckets. A well-designed navigation system can make all the difference in creating a seamless and enjoyable user experience.

Let's look at some examples of navigation in different docs' sites. Figure 4-12 shows that TypeScript docs have closed/expanding icons large enough for different finger sizes, and the individual menu items are easily clickable.

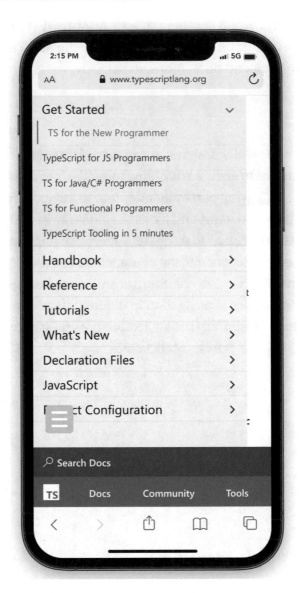

Figure 4-12. *TypeScript docs example of mobile menu sizing*

The Kotlin docs, as we see in Figure 4-13, have a font on the menu that is too small, but the button height feels sufficient.

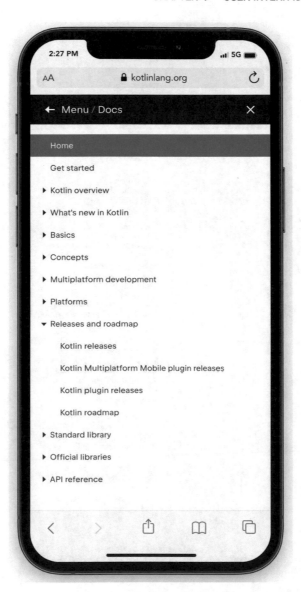

Figure 4-13. *Kotlin docs example of mobile menu sizing*

The Ruby docs, as shown in Figure 4-14, do not have a great navigation menu, making it extremely difficult for community members to navigate the menu topics in both the main and left-hand navigation.

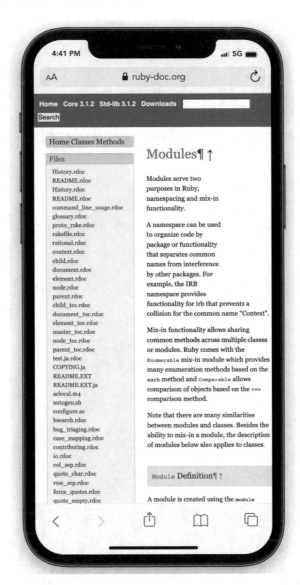

Figure 4-14. *Ruby docs example of mobile menu sizing*

Figure 4-15 from AsyncAPI docs shows menu items with a short description, making it easier for community members of any finger size to easily click on their link of choice. Having clear labeling for your main docs' menu and sub-menu is important. In Figure 4-16 from AsyncAPI docs, the docs menu and sub-menu are easily visible, with the sub-menu items linking to their chosen content buckets.

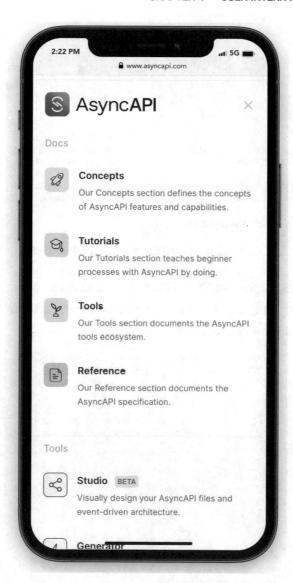

Figure 4-15. *AsyncAPI docs example of mobile menu sizing*

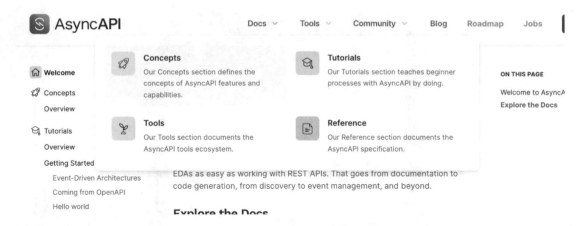

Figure 4-16. *AsyncAPI docs sub-menu and navigation items*

On the other hand, Figure 4-17 from Gitpod docs lacks a sub-menu clarifying their main content division. Still, they include a docs menu item in their main navigation, making it easy for community members to find them.

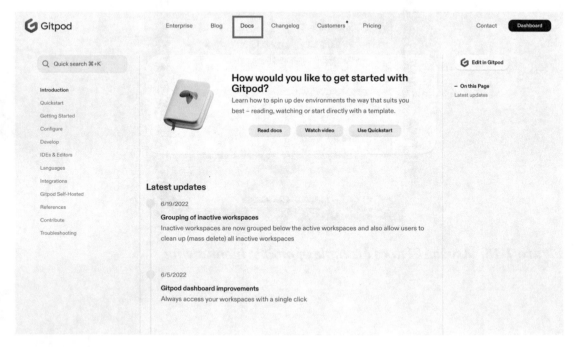

Figure 4-17. *Gitpod docs menu item in their navigation*

An example of what happens when you do not clearly label your main docs' menu or sub-menu can be seen on the ReadMe website via Figure 4-18, which has both a *Product* and *Learn* menu item, each with a sub-menu item for documentation.

It can be confusing for community members to determine which docs link to visit first, and the reasoning behind having multiple options is unclear, as seen in Figures 4-19 to 4-21.

Figure 4-18. *The ReadMe website has a **Product** menu with a sub-menu item titled "Documentation"*

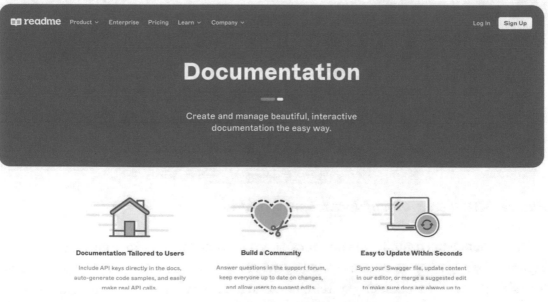

Figure 4-19. *Screenshot of readme.com/documentation*

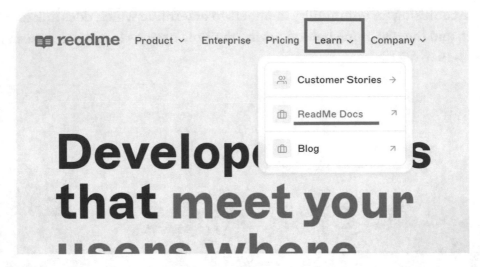

Figure 4-20. *ReadMe website has a **Learn** menu with a sub-menu item titled "ReadMe Docs"*

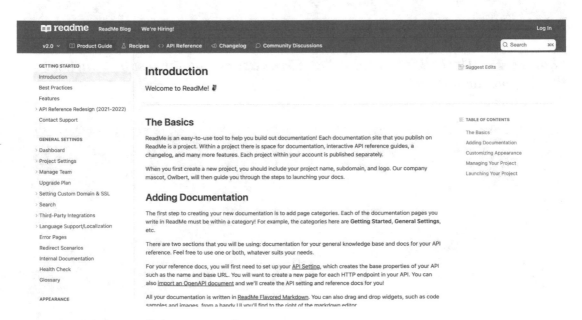

Figure 4-21. *Screenshot of docs.readme.com/docs*

To enhance the usability of your docs' site, it is crucial to prioritize clear and organized navigation. As demonstrated by the preceding examples, mobile menu items, font sizing, and a clear labeling system for menu items significantly impact the user experience. Ensuring your navigation is easy to use helps community members find the information they need quickly and efficiently, resulting in a more positive experience overall.

Search

Including a search bar on your docs' site is essential to providing a great user experience. Community members appreciate being able to quickly and efficiently find information. When implementing a search bar, indexing your content appropriately and optimizing the search performance are crucial.

Here are some best UX practices for docs' search bars:

1. **Place the search bar in a prominent location:** Place the docs search bar in a prominent location; ideally, it should be located at the top of the page and be easily accessible from any page.

2. **Implement autocomplete:** Autocomplete saves time and effort by suggesting popular or related search terms as community members type queries in the search bar.

3. **Provide clear feedback:** The search bar should highlight the search terms in the search results, display the number of search results, and provide a clear indication if no search results are found.

4. **Optimize search results:** Provide clear and concise titles and descriptions.

5. **Test and optimize:** Ask community members to identify issues or pain points.

Let's look at some search examples from a couple of docs' sites. One of my favorite implementations of a docs search bar can be found in Django docs. In Figure 4-22, you can see how Django's search bar performs queries quickly and content displayed in search results is effectively optimized.

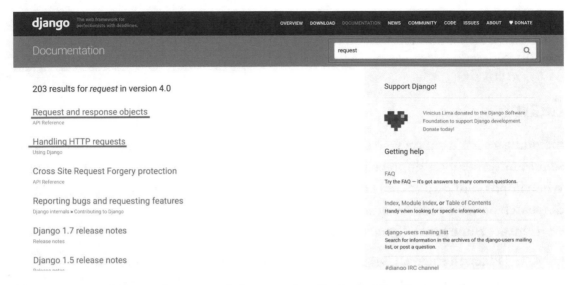

Figure 4-22. *Django docs search bar results displayed for "request"*

Another example to consider is Oracle Java docs, shown in Figure 4-23, where we see a delayed performance and the search results take longer to load. It's never a good sign when community members face the three spinning dots of death; at that point, they might as well take a coffee break while waiting for the results to load! Proper indexing is crucial to providing your community with a smooth and efficient docs search experience.

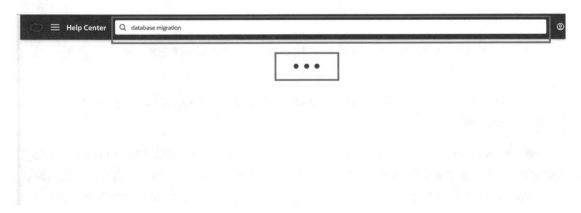

Figure 4-23. *Oracle Java docs search bar lags in displaying search results for "database migration"*

Diagrams

Diagrams are a visually appealing way of conveying complex information. When it comes to creating diagrams for your docs, there are numerous software and tool options available. Select the option that suits your preferences and needs.

One free option to consider is Figma FigJam, which allows you to create diagrams of user flows, processes, systems, and more with its drag-and-drop interface. Their user-friendly interface provides a seamless experience for those who prefer a designer-focused interface.

Another option is MermaidJS, a JavaScript library that enables you to create and modify diagrams through Markdown syntax. MermaidJS is a powerful tool for those who prefer working with code and offers more customization options. (It's worth noting that the UML diagrams included in this book were created using Mermaid syntax, demonstrating its versatility and ease of use.)

Regardless of your chosen tool, ensure your diagrams are clear, concise, and easy to understand. Use colors, shapes, and labels to make the information more visually appealing and accessible.

Figure 4-24 showcases Figma FigJam's Diagramming feature, demonstrating its ease of use and drag-and-drop interface.

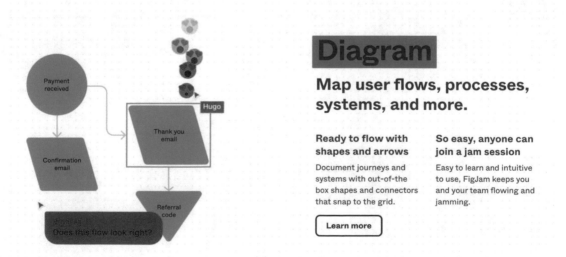

Figure 4-24. *FigJam home page card detailing their Diagramming feature*

The examples in Figures 4-25 and 4-26 demonstrate how MermaidJS can be used to create Class Diagrams with Markdown syntax.

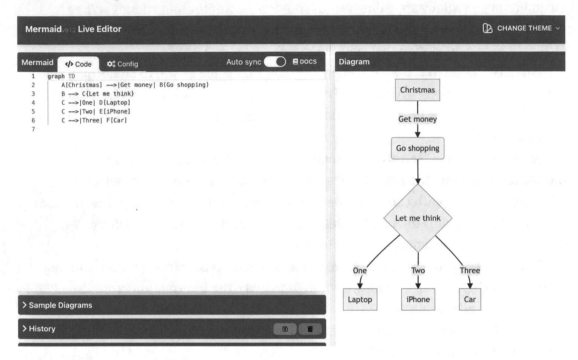

Figure 4-25. *MermaidJS Live Editor[6]*

---

[6] https://mermaid-js.github.io/mermaid-live-editor/

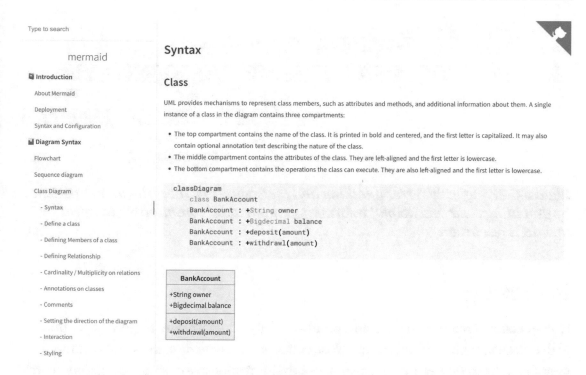

Figure 4-26. *MermaidJS Markdown syntax example for Class Diagrams[7]*

Error Handling and Messaging

Effective error handling and messaging improves the user experience by providing clear and helpful information that guides community members toward a resolution. It can also reduce frustration and confusion, leading to a better overall experience with the product, as noted in Figure 4-27.

In documentation, error messages should be concise, easy to understand, and specific to the issue at hand, provide actionable steps to resolve the issue, and provide links to additional resources for more information.

Designers play an important role in the development of error handling and messaging. They can work with technical writers and developers to create user-friendly error messages that are visually appealing and consistent with the overall design and branding of the project. Designers can also ensure that error messages are accessible to community members with different needs, such as those who use screen readers or other assistive technologies.

---

[7]https://mermaid-js.github.io/mermaid/#/classDiagram

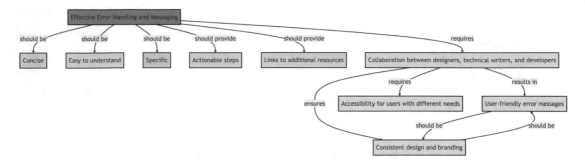

Figure 4-27. *Effective error handling and messaging improves the user experience by providing clear and helpful information that guides community members toward a resolution*

In Closing

In conclusion, creating a user-friendly and accessible docs website requires attention to detail, clear communication, and close collaboration with designers and community members. Focus on key areas such as accessibility, responsive design, navigation, search functionality, and error handling. Create a documentation site that enhances the user experience and facilitates effective communication between community members.

Now that we have explored the fundamental concepts of UX/UI design in docs, it's time to shift our focus to the next chapter on documenting APIs. Get ready to dive into the essential practices for documenting APIs and learn how to create API documentation that is both comprehensive and accessible.

CHAPTER 5

Documenting APIs

In this chapter, we'll explore the important topic of *Documenting APIs (Application Programming Interfaces)*.

The API documentation process encompasses various stages, such as design, writing, editing, and testing, as shown in Figure 5-1. We'll focus on documenting REST APIs and cover key elements such as parameters, endpoints, code examples, requests, responses, status error codes, and authentication. Understanding the structure and content of API documentation is essential for effectively communicating an API's functionality and usage. Additionally, we will explore API docs testing tools and techniques to validate API functionality, performance, and security. We'll also discuss the collaborative nature of API documentation and the importance of shared ownership between technical writers and engineers.

© Alejandra Quetzalli 2023
A. Quetzalli, *Docs-as-Ecosystem*, https://doi.org/10.1007/978-1-4842-9328-7_5

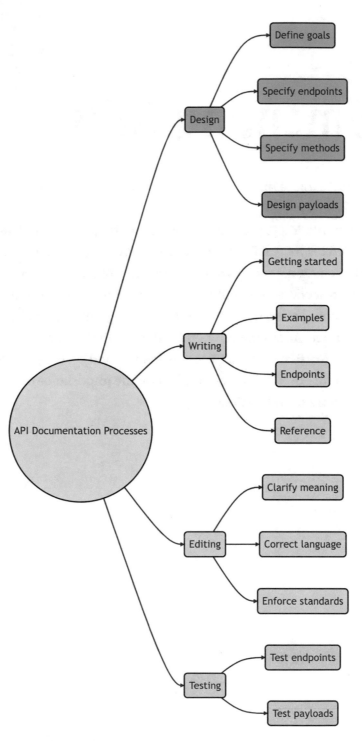

Figure 5-1. *The API documentation process encompasses various stages such as design, writing, editing, and testing*

Why the Need?

APIs are essential for enabling communication and interaction between software applications. They provide a standardized way for applications to exchange data and perform various operations. API documentation is crucial for understanding and integrating an API effectively, as discussed in Figure 5-2. It reduces the learning curve, boosts productivity, and promotes API adoption. Documentation showcases the API's features, functionality, and use cases, helping developers assess its value and integrate it into their applications. It also serves as a valuable resource for troubleshooting and support, offering solutions to common issues and enabling quick problem resolution.

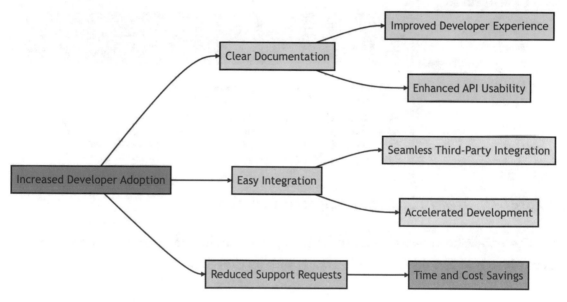

Figure 5-2.   *The value of documenting APIs*

Structuring API Docs

Structuring API documentation is crucial for organizing and presenting content in a logical and user-friendly manner. To begin your API documentation, provide an overview summarizing your API and its purpose (Figure 5-3). Your API overview should highlight the problem your API solves and its benefits compared to similar APIs.

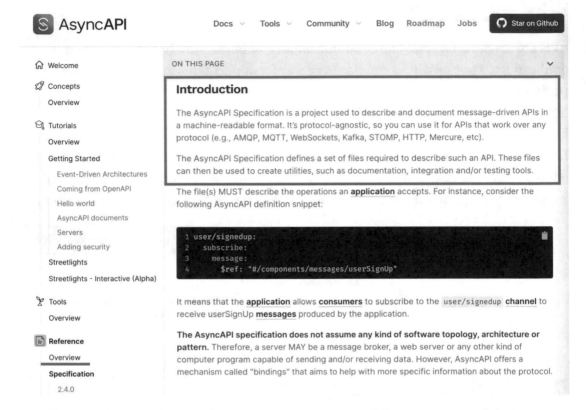

Figure 5-3. *AsyncAPI Specification* ***overview*** *example[1]*

Figure 5-4 showcases a Create a Coupon API example from Stripe Docs, a second example of how API documentation starts with an overview.

---

[1] www.asyncapi.com/docs/reference/specification/v2.4.0#introduction

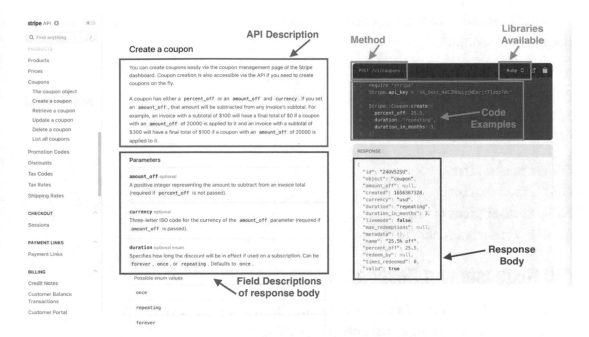

Figure 5-4. *"Create a Coupon" API documentation example from Stripe Docs[2]*

Organizing by Functionality or Endpoint

One effective approach to organizing API documentation is to structure it based on functionality or endpoint (Figure 5-5), allowing for a logical grouping of documentation based on each endpoint's specific feature or action.

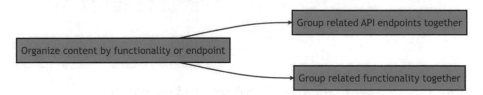

Figure 5-5. *Organize API content by functionality or endpoint*

---

[2] https://stripe.com/docs/api/coupons/create

To illustrate this concept, let's consider a hypothetical banking API documentation organized by endpoint:

```
GET /accounts
POST /accounts
PUT /accounts/:id
DELETE /accounts/:id

GET /transactions
POST /transactions
PUT /transactions/:id
DELETE /transactions/:id
```

API Requests and Responses

API documentation should provide clear and detailed information about how to make requests and what responses to expect (Figure 5-6).

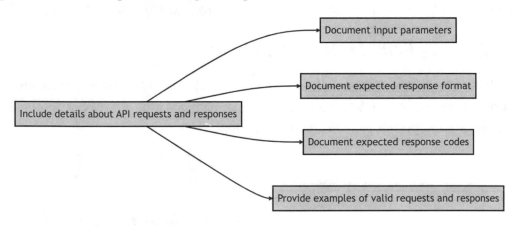

Figure 5-6. *Include details about API requests and responses*

For requests, the documentation should outline the HTTP methods supported by the API, such as GET, POST, PUT, and DELETE, and specify the corresponding endpoints for each action. Documenting responses from the API includes specifying the response format, such as JSON or XML, and explaining the structure and meaning of the data returned. Remember to outline possible status codes and their meanings, such as 200 for a successful response, 404 for resource not found, or 500 for server errors.

Let's build on our hypothetical banking example and showcase a request and response:

```
Endpoint: /accounts
Method: POST
Request Body:
{
  "name": "Jane Doe",
  "balance": 500.00
}
Response Body:
{
  "id": "1234",
  "name": "Jane Doe",
  "balance": 500.00
}
```

API Versioning and Release Notes

APIs are updated and improved over time. It's important to document the changes made to the API and indicate the current version (Figure 5-7) by adding a version number to the API endpoint or a version header in the request.

Here's an example of versioning our banking API using a version header:

```
GET /accounts
Accept-Version: 1.0
```

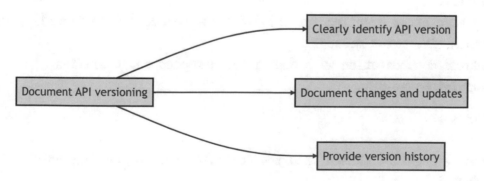

Figure 5-7. *Document API versioning*

Use **API Release Notes** to document the changes made in each API version, including any modifications to existing endpoints, the introduction of new endpoints, changes in request/response formats, deprecations, and bug fixes. They provide developers with a clear understanding of what has been added, modified, or removed, enabling them to adapt their integrations accordingly.

Here's an example API Release Note:

```
API v2.1.0 Release Notes
=========================
Date: May 15, 2023

Summary
-------
In this release, we introduce several new features, enhancements, and bug
fixes to improve the functionality and performance of our API.

New Features
------------
1. /users endpoint now supports pagination for improved performance.
2. Introducing a new /order endpoint to retrieve order information.
3. Added support for webhooks to receive real-time updates on user
   activities.

Enhancements
------------
1. Improved response time for the /products endpoint by optimizing database
   queries.
2. Enhanced error handling for invalid input parameters to provide more
   informative error messages.
3. Updated documentation with additional examples and clarified
   endpoint usage.

Bug Fixes
---------
1. Fixed a bug that caused incorrect calculations in the /payments
   endpoint.
2. Resolved an issue with the /inventory endpoint returning
   inconsistent data.
```

```
Breaking Changes
----------------
None

Deprecations
------------
None
```

Please refer to the API documentation for detailed information about these changes and how to adapt your integrations accordingly.

If you have any questions or need further assistance, please don't hesitate to contact our support team.

Thank you for using our API!

API Authentication

APIs often require authentication to access sensitive data or perform certain actions. API documentation should clearly explain the authentication process and requirements (Figure 5-8) via example authentication headers or using OAuth flows.

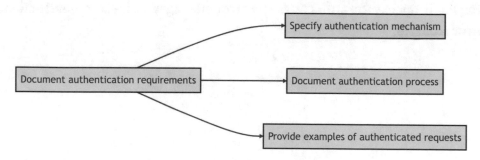

Figure 5-8. *Document authentication requirements*

Here's an example of documenting our banking API's authentication process:

```
Endpoint: /accounts/:id
Method: PUT
Authentication: Bearer Token
```

```
Request Body:
{
  "name": "John Doe",
  "balance": 750.00
}
```

Testing API Docs and Error Handling

Testing API documentation is crucial to ensure the accuracy and effectiveness of the documentation itself. It involves verifying that the documented API functionalities, parameters, and responses align with the actual behavior of the API. Follow a systematic approach to test API documentation effectively (Figure 5-9). Review the documentation to ensure it is comprehensive and accurate. Set up a dedicated test environment that mimics the production environment. Define and execute test scenarios that cover various use cases and potential errors. Validate the actual API responses against the expected results documented in the API documentation. Report any discrepancies or errors found during the testing process.

Error handling is another vital aspect to address in the API documentation. It is essential to document potential errors during API interactions and provide guidance on handling them. Specify the error codes and error messages and recommend actions for each error scenario.

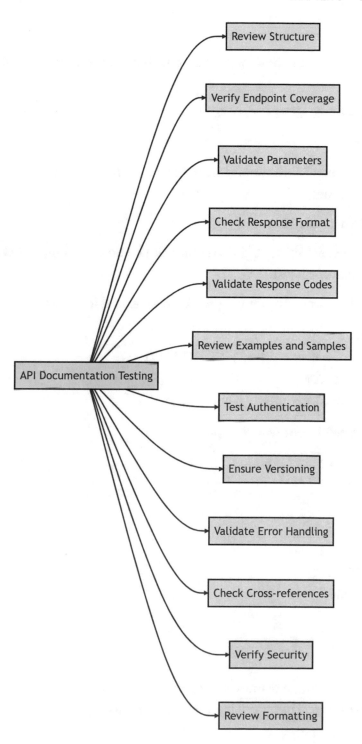

Figure 5-9. *Steps in the API documentation process*

Testing

Let's test the API documentation for our example banking API with the following structure:

- **Testing bank API:** Account balance

- **Endpoint:** `"/api/balance"`.

- **Description:** This endpoint retrieves the current balance of a user's bank account.

- **HTTP method:** GET.

- **Parameters:** `"account_id"` (required): The unique identifier of the user's bank account.

Here's what that structure would look like in an example code snippet:

```
Request Example:
GET /api/balance?account_id=123456 HTTP/1.1
Host: api.example.com
Authorization: Bearer <access_token>
```

Here's a successful response example:

```
- HTTP Status Code: 200 (OK)
- Response Body:
```json
{
  "account_id": "123456",
  "balance": 2500.00,
  "currency": "USD"
}
```

Error Handling

If the `account_id` parameter is missing or invalid, the API will return a 400 (Bad Request) status code. The response body will include an error message specifying the issue.
```

Error Handling Example:

```
GET /api/balance?account_id=invalid HTTP/1.1
Host: api.example.com
Authorization: Bearer <access_token>
```

Response Example:

```
HTTP/1.1 400 Bad Request
Content-Type: application/json
{
  "error": "Invalid account_id",
  "message": "The provided account_id parameter is not valid."
}
```

In this example, a request is made to the "/api/balance" endpoint with an invalid "account_id" parameter. The API responds with a "400 Bad Request" status code, indicating a client error. The response body includes an error message that specifies the issue, helping developers understand the cause of the error.

Tools for Testing and Documenting APIs

Tools for testing and documenting APIs play a crucial role in ensuring the quality and accuracy of API documentation. Here are a few popular API testing tools that can greatly aid your API technical writing efforts:

1. **Postman:** Postman is a widely used tool for testing and documenting APIs (Figure 5-10). It provides a user-friendly interface for creating and saving collections of requests. Postman offers features such as automatic documentation generation and viewing and analyzing response data. It serves as a comprehensive platform for building and maintaining APIs.

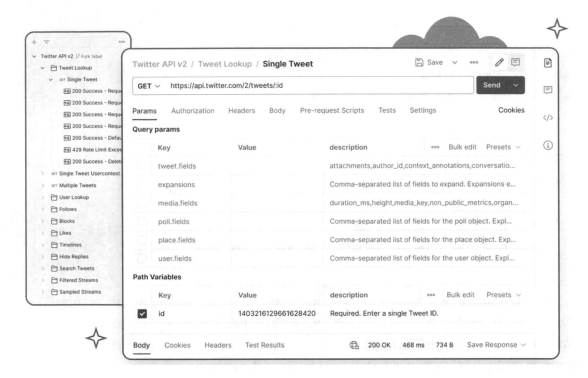

Figure 5-10. *Image from the Postman website showcasing the Postman API client, which is the foundation of the Postman platform*

2. **AsyncAPI Studio:** AsyncAPI Studio is a powerful tool that allows you to develop an Open Source Software (OSS) AsyncAPI document (Figure 5-11). It provides functionalities for validating the document, converting it to the latest version, previewing the documentation, and visualizing asynchronous events in event-driven architectures (EDAs).

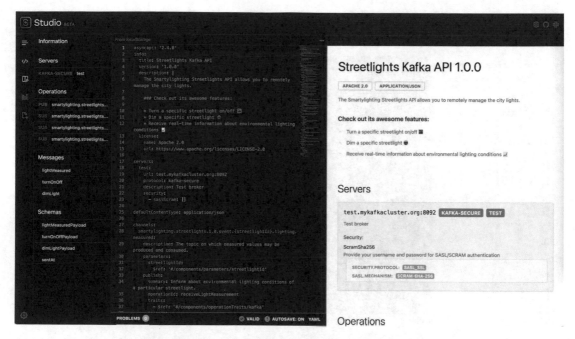

Figure 5-11. *AsyncAPI Studio tool for developing and visualizing asynchronous event-driven architectures*

3. **SwaggerHub:** SwaggerHub is an integrated API development platform designed for the Swagger (OpenAPI) framework (Figure 5-12). It offers capabilities for building, documenting, managing, and deploying APIs. SwaggerHub streamlines the API documentation process and provides a collaborative environment for teams working on API projects.

Figure 5-12. *SwaggerHub tool for building, documenting, managing, and deploying APIs*

More Resources

To further expand your knowledge and skills in API technical writing, I highly recommend the following API documentation tutorials:

- **"I'd Rather Be Writing: API Documentation Course":** This comprehensive course offers in-depth guidance on writing effective API documentation. It covers various topics such as API design, documentation standards, tooling, and best practices.[3]

- **"Write the Docs: Developer Documentation and APIs":** This tutorial from Write the Docs provides valuable insights into developer documentation and API writing. It delves into strategies for creating clear and concise API documentation that meets the needs of developers.[4]

---

[3] https://idratherbewriting.com/learnapidoc

[4] www.writethedocs.org/guide/#api-documentation and www.writethedocs.org/guide/writing/style-guides/#developer-documentation-and-apis

- **"I'd Rather Be Writing: Documenting GraphQL APIs":** This tutorial specifically focuses on documenting GraphQL APIs. It offers practical tips and techniques for documenting GraphQL schemas, queries, mutations, and subscriptions.[5]

- **"How to Write API Documentation: Alex Soft's Best Practices and Examples":** This resource provides a collection of best practices and real-world examples for writing API documentation. It covers essential topics such as API structure, request/response examples, authentication, and error handling.[6]

Who Owns API Docs?

A common question that arises in API documentation is determining ownership. Should it be the responsibility of engineers or technical writers? A collaborative approach can provide the best outcome, where engineers and technical writers share ownership of API docs, as shown in Figure 5-13. Whether working in a product-oriented organization or an Open Source Software (OSS) community, a balanced approach is key, with technical writers and engineers playing essential roles as core maintainers and code owners in API docs repositories.

Engineers should take the lead in updating API docs with each release, ensuring the documentation accurately reflects the latest changes. However, it is important to involve technical writers in the process. Before merging, technical writers can review and approve pull requests (PRs) related to API documentation, ensuring the documentation meets quality standards, consistency, and clarity. Adopting a shared ownership model means technical writers and engineers share responsibilities in maintaining API documentation.

---

[5] https://idratherbewriting.com/learnapidoc/docapis_graphql_apis.html
[6] www.altexsoft.com/blog/api-documentation/

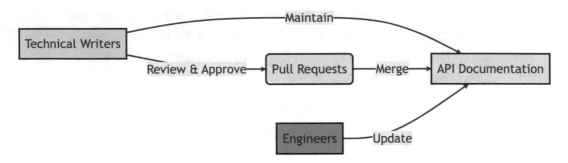

Figure 5-13. *In a shared ownership model, technical writers and engineers contribute to maintaining the API documentation, each with their respective responsibilities*

In Closing

In this chapter, we explored the fundamental aspects of documenting APIs. We discussed the importance of well-structured API documentation, including organizing content, documenting API requests and responses, versioning, authentication, testing, and error handling. We also highlighted the shared ownership of API documentation, emphasizing the collaboration between technical writers and engineers. Remember that sharing responsibilities and maintaining a strong partnership with diverse stakeholders ensure both parties contribute their expertise for creating effective API documentation.

Get ready for the next chapter, an exciting journey into documenting SDKs!

CHAPTER 6

Documenting SDKs

In this chapter, I will introduce the subject of *Documenting Software Development Kits (SDKs)*. SDKs are software tools, libraries, and documentation used to create applications for a specific platform or framework. SDKs provide pre-built functionality, APIs, and development resources for streamlining the app development process. They typically include programming language support, sample code, debugging tools, and other utilities that assist community members in building, testing, and integrating their software applications.

Throughout this chapter, we will cover a range of topics (Figure 6-1), including the structuring of SDK documentation, providing clear installation and setup guides, offering detailed usage and integration instructions, creating comprehensive references, showcasing tutorials with code examples, and highlighting the importance of release notes. We'll also discuss the ownership of SDK documentation and share additional resources to enhance your understanding further.

© Alejandra Quetzalli 2023
A. Quetzalli, *Docs-as-Ecosystem*, https://doi.org/10.1007/978-1-4842-9328-7_6

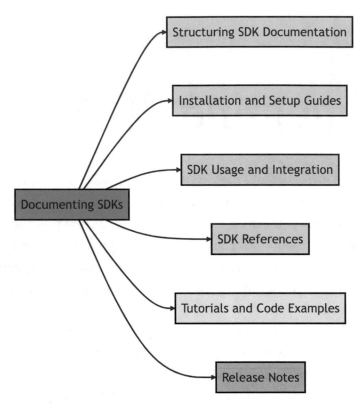

Figure 6-1. *Steps in documenting SDKs*

Hoist the sails and get ready to embark on this exhilarating voyage into the world of documenting SDKs (Figure 6-2)!

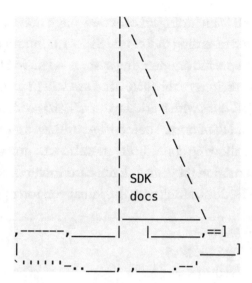

Figure 6-2. ASCII (American Standard Code for Information Interchange) art of a sailboat with a sail that reads "SDK docs"

Why the Need?

Ask anyone what kind of documentation can make you sleep faster, and I guarantee the response you'll often get is SDK docs! It's no secret that SDK documentation can be a snooze-fest. But here's the thing: despite their reputation for inducing drowsiness, SDK docs are an essential resource for community members. They provide crucial information on how to use SDKs effectively and integrate them into our applications.

However, the challenge lies in making SDK documentation engaging and community friendly. Community members should be able to easily grasp the concepts, understand the SDK's features and functionalities, and quickly find the necessary information.

Adopting a community-centric approach and implementing best practices in SDK documentation will transform those sleep-inducing SDK docs into valuable resources that community members enjoy reading. So let's roll up our sleeves, wake up those SDK docs, and make them as lively and engaging as possible!

Structuring SDK Documentation

Structuring SDK documentation is critical to creating an intuitive, user-friendly experience for community members.

One effective approach is including an overview page that utilizes a grid layout with rows of cards, each representing individual SDKs maintained.[1] These cards should provide links to language-specific or operating system-specific SDKs. Remember to include links to previous versions of the SDKs that are still in use.

A great example of SDK docs with a grid layout of cards can be seen in Figure 6-3, showcasing Stripe Terminal SDK docs. Their design utilizes a simple and clean grid layout with rows of cards, allowing community members to quickly and easily identify the relevant SDK documentation they need. Each card includes a brief description of the content covered in the SDK docs, along with the latest version of the SDK.

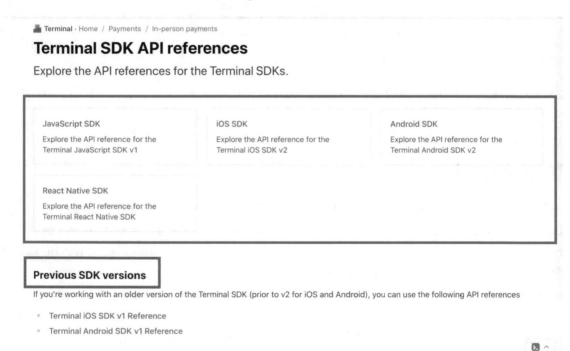

Figure 6-3. *Stripe Terminal SDK docs exemplify a grid layout with cards, providing a well-organized and user-friendly outline for easily locating specific SDK documentation[2]*

---

[1] Replicating the grid cards idea for SDK documentation can be accomplished using various tools and technologies, including documentation platforms like ReadMe and Swagger UI, static site generators such as Jekyll and Hugo, component libraries like React and Vue.js, and CSS frameworks like Bootstrap and Bulma.

[2] https://stripe.com/docs/terminal/references/api

Combining a grid layout, descriptive information, and easy navigation helps community members locate the specific SDK documentation they require, enhancing their overall experience and efficiency.

Installation and Setup

Installation and setup instructions are crucial components of SDK documentation. The installation and setup section should outline the prerequisites, such as supported platforms, dependencies, and any additional libraries or tools required.

To smooth the installation process, provide step-by-step instructions that are easy to follow. Consider including code snippets that demonstrate the installation commands for various package managers, such as npm or pip, depending on the SDK language or framework.

Here's an example of installation instructions for a hypothetical banking SDK using an npm package manager:

1. Ensure you have Node.js installed on your system.

2. Open your terminal or command prompt.

3. Run the following command to install the SDK package:

   ```
   npm install sdk-bank-customer-accounts
   ```

4. Once the installation is complete, you can import the SDK into your project using the following JavaScript code snippet:

   ```
   const SDK = require('sdk-bank-customer-accounts');
   ```

SDK Usage Guide

An SDK Usage Guide provides instructions to utilize an SDK's features and functionalities in applications. Remember to cover the various methods, classes, and APIs provided by the SDK, along with code snippet examples that demonstrate how to perform common tasks or interact with specific functionalities of the SDK. Clear explanations and annotations should accompany these code snippets to help community members understand the purpose and flow of the code.

Here's a usage guide and code snippet example of a hypothetical banking SDK in Node.js that retrieves a customer's account balance:

```
const bankingSDK = require('banking-sdk');

// Initialize the SDK with your API credentials
const sdk = new bankingSDK.SDK({ apiKey: 'YOUR_API_KEY', apiSecret: 'YOUR_
API_SECRET' });

// Retrieve the account balance for a customer
const customerId = 'CUSTOMER_ID';
const accountBalance = sdk.getAccountBalance(customerId);

// Display the account balance
console.log(`Account Balance for Customer ${customerId}:
${accountBalance}`);
```

In this example, we require the banking SDK and create an instance of it by initializing it with the required API key and secret. We then use the SDK's getAccountBalance() method to retrieve the account balance for a specific customer identified by their customer ID. The account balance is stored in the accountBalance variable, and we display it in the console.

This code snippet demonstrates how community members can use the banking SDK in Node.js to interact with banking APIs and retrieve account balance information for customers easily.

SDK Integration Guide

An SDK Integration Guide offers guidance on the necessary setup, configuration, and implementation steps to ensure a smooth integration process.

An effective SDK integration guide should include the following elements:

- **Prerequisites**: Outline any prerequisites or dependencies required for integrating the SDK, such as minimum software versions or additional libraries.

- **Installation**: Provide detailed instructions on installing and setting up the SDK in the developer's environment, including any specific package managers or installation commands.

- **Configuration**: Explain how to configure the SDK, such as setting up API credentials or authentication tokens and additional configuration options available.

- **Initialization**: Show how to initialize the SDK in an application, including code snippets.

- **Basic usage**: Provide example code snippets that illustrate the basic usage of the SDK, such as making simple API requests or accessing common functionality.

- **Advanced features**: If the SDK offers advanced features or capabilities, include code snippets and explanations on utilizing them effectively.

- **Troubleshooting**: Detail common troubleshooting errors, with guidance on debugging and resolving them.

Here's an example code snippet for an SDK Integration Guide:

```javascript
const myApp = require('my-app');
const mySdk = require('my-sdk');

// Initialize SDK
mySdk.initialize();

// Setup API credentials
mySdk.setCredentials('API_KEY', 'API_SECRET');

// Configure additional options
mySdk.configure({
  debugMode: true,
  timeout: 5000,
});

// Perform simple API request
mySdk.makeRequest('GET', '/api/data', (response) => {
  console.log('Response:', response);
});
```

```
// Access advanced features
const advancedFeature = mySdk.getAdvancedFeature('featureName');
advancedFeature.enable();

// Handle errors and exceptions
try {
  mySdk.doSomething();
} catch (error) {
  console.error('Error:', error);
}
```

In this example, we demonstrate the integration of a hypothetical SDK into a Node. js application. The code snippet includes steps for initializing the SDK, setting up API credentials, configuring additional options, making an API request, accessing advanced features, and handling errors.

SDK Reference

SDK Reference documentation is a comprehensive guide for understanding an SDK's capabilities and how to utilize them in applications. In SDK Reference documentation, each class, method, or property is typically documented separately, providing information on its purpose, input parameters, return values, and any additional details relevant to its usage. It is important to provide clear and concise explanations and code snippet examples to illustrate how each component should be used.

Here's an example of a code snippet from an SDK Reference documentation for a banking SDK that demonstrates the usage of a method to transfer funds between two bank accounts:

```
/**
 * Transfers funds from one bank account to another.
 * @param {string} fromAccount - The ID of the account to transfer
   funds from.
 * @param {string} toAccount - The ID of the account to transfer funds to.
 * @param {number} amount - The amount to transfer.
 * @returns {Promise<boolean>} - A Promise that resolves to true if the
   transfer is successful.
 * @throws {Error} - If the transfer fails or the account IDs are invalid.
 */
```

```
async function transferFunds(fromAccount, toAccount, amount) {
  // Implementation code to transfer funds between accounts
  // ...
  return true;
}
```

In this example, the `transferFunds` method is documented with JSDoc comments. It specifies the input parameters `fromAccount`, `toAccount`, and `amount`, along with their respective types. It also mentions the return value as a `Promise` that resolves to a boolean indicating the success of the transfer. Additionally, it notes the possibility of throwing an `Error` if the transfer fails or the account IDs are invalid.

This documentation provides the necessary information to correctly use the "transferFunds" method, including the expected input parameters, return value, and potential error scenarios.

SDK Tutorials and Code Examples

SDK tutorials and code examples help community members grasp and utilize an SDK effectively. SDK tutorials offer beginner step-by-step instructions showcasing leveraging different SDK features and functionalities. On the other hand, code examples demonstrate real-world use cases and illustrate how to solve common problems using the SDK. Provide clear explanations, step-by-step instructions, and well-annotated code snippets.

Best practices for SDK tutorial coverage typically include the following:

1. **Getting started tutorial:** Get acquainted with the SDK's basic functionalities.

2. **Authentication tutorials:** Cover the process of authenticating an application, the necessary credentials or access tokens, the authentication flow, best practices for securing authentication, and examples of making authenticated API requests using the SDK.

3. **Error handling tutorials:** Explain common error scenarios, error codes, validation errors, and how to handle errors gracefully.

4. **Advanced features tutorials:** Explore specific use cases, demonstrate advanced API requests, and showcase advanced functionalities. Explore the SDK's full potential and discover additional features to enhance applications.

SDK Release Notes

SDK Release Notes provide information about the additions, improvements, bug fixes, deprecations, and breaking changes in a structured manner. They should be concise yet informative, highlighting the key changes and their impact. Including version numbers, release dates, and any necessary migration or upgrade instructions is also beneficial.

Here's an example of an SDK Release Note:

```
-------------------------------------------------
SDK Release Notes - Version 2.0.0
-------------------------------------------------

New Features:
- Added support for multi-threading, improving performance in multi-core
  environments.
- Introduced a new module for real-time data streaming, allowing seamless
  integration with streaming services.
- Implemented a comprehensive caching mechanism to optimize data retrieval
  and reduce network overhead.
- Added compatibility with the latest version of the XYZ API, enabling
  access to new API endpoints and features.

Enhancements:
- Improved error handling and error messages for better debugging and
  troubleshooting.
- Optimized memory management, reducing memory footprint and improving
  efficiency.
- Streamlined the authentication process, providing simpler and more secure
  authentication methods.
- Added comprehensive documentation with code examples and usage guidelines
  for easier integration and development.
```

Bug Fixes:
- Resolved a critical issue causing crashes in certain edge cases when handling large datasets.
- Fixed a memory leak during long-running operations, leading to performance degradation.
- Addressed a compatibility issue with older operating systems, ensuring backward compatibility.

Deprecations:
- Deprecated the legacy authentication method. Users are encouraged to migrate to the new authentication flow.

Breaking Changes:
- Changed the response structure for the get_user endpoint. Refer to the updated documentation for the new response format.

Who Owns SDK Docs?

Promoting collaboration and shared ownership between engineers and technical writers helps organizations ensure their SDK docs are regularly updated, remain accurate, and provide a positive community experience. Collaboration bridges the gap between technical implementation and effective communication, resulting in high-quality SDK documentation.

Engineers play a crucial role in updating the SDK docs with each release. They are responsible for incorporating changes, adding new features, and providing technical insights. However, it is important to have the involvement of technical writers to review and approve pull requests[3] (PRs) before merging them into the documentation, as seen in Figure 6-4. A collaborative model ensures SDK documentation is accurate, clear, and consistent with the intended messaging.

---

[3] "Pull requests" (PRs) is a term from GitHub, a popular code version control system. It represents a proposed code change or addition submitted for review by community members. Other code version management systems, such as GitLab and Bitbucket, may use different terminology for the same concept. For example, GitLab uses "Merge Requests" (MRs), while Bitbucket uses "pull requests" as well.

In this paradigm, the responsibility for maintaining the SDK docs is shared equally between technical writers and engineers, each with its responsibilities. Engineers contribute their technical expertise and knowledge of the SDK, while technical writers bring expertise in crafting clear and user-friendly documentation. Together, they create a cohesive and comprehensive SDK documentation that meets the needs of community members using the SDK.

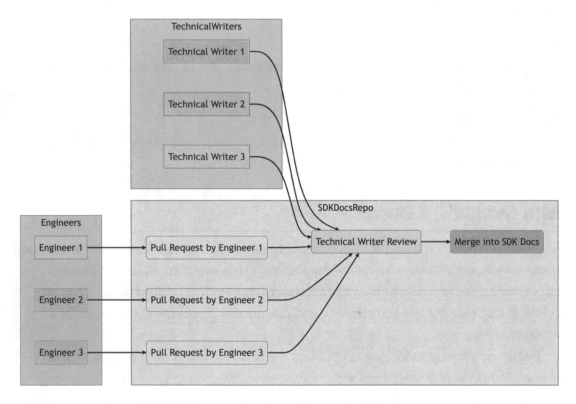

Figure 6-4. *The collaborative ownership of SDK docs between engineers and technical writers*

More Resources

Visit the following resource to continue your education in SDK documentation:

- I'd Rather Be Writing: SDK docs tutorial[4]

---

[4] https://idratherbewriting.com/learnapidoc/docapis_sdks.html

In Closing

In this chapter, we delved into the importance of structuring community-friendly SDK docs, catering to community members of all levels. We discussed following best practices, such as providing code examples, addressing common use cases, and offering troubleshooting guidance. We also emphasized the importance of shared ownership in maintaining SDK docs, encouraging collaboration between engineers and technical writers so that SDK documentation can benefit from the combined expertise and perspectives of both parties.

Let's head over to the next chapter where we'll unlock the potential of integrating docs into CI/CD pipelines and harness the benefits of automated documentation processes.

CHAPTER 7

Integrating Docs into CI/CD Pipelines

In this chapter, I will introduce the subject of *Integrating Documentation into Continuous Integration/Continuous Delivery (CI/CD) Pipelines*. The CI concept focuses on frequently integrating code changes into a shared repository. It involves automatically building and testing the code to identify any issues early in the development cycle. CI helps prevent integration conflicts and ensures the stability of the software by continuously integrating code changes from multiple community members. CD furthers the concept by automating software deployment to various environments: development, staging, and production. It enables frequent and reliable software releases, ensuring that updates and new features reach end users quickly and efficiently.

Thinking of documentation as an ecosystem brings a broader perspective to how we approach integrating documentation into CI/CD pipelines. We can reframe documentation as an integral part of the ecosystem rather than a separate entity or an afterthought in the software development process by emphasizing its significant impact on technology or product adoption (Figure 7-1).

© Alejandra Quetzalli 2023
A. Quetzalli, *Docs-as-Ecosystem*, https://doi.org/10.1007/978-1-4842-9328-7_7

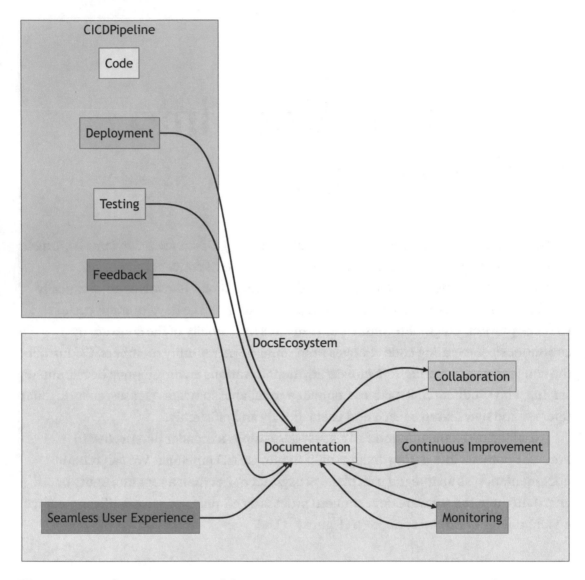

Figure 7-1. *The integration of documentation as an ecosystem into CI/CD pipelines*

The ensuing chapter will delve into several key aspects of integrating documentation into CI/CD pipelines by adopting an ecosystem mindset. We will explore treating documentation as code, enabling version control, collaboration, and automation. Additionally, we will discuss the importance of continuous improvement in documentation, fostering iterative enhancements, and incorporating community feedback. Community collaboration and feedback processes will be highlighted, emphasizing the benefits of involving diverse stakeholders across the community.

Why the Need?

When integrating documentation into CI/CD pipelines (Figure 7-2), adopting an ecosystem mindset is crucial, especially when considering the community members involved. Treating documentation as an integral part of the software development ecosystem recognizes its impact on community engagement, adoption, and overall success.

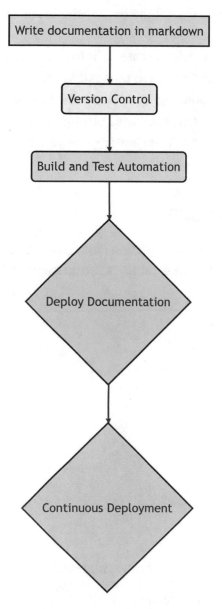

Figure 7-2. *Integrating docs into CI/CD pipeline processes*

An ecosystem mindset influences integration by emphasizing collaboration, continuous improvement, and feedback loops. It encourages community members, including developers and technical writers, to collaborate closely. Collaboration ensures that documentation aligns with the latest software updates, while continuous improvement allows for iterative updates based on community feedback. Community feedback loops, facilitated through mechanisms like pull requests[1] and review processes, enable community members to contribute their insights and ensure documentation accuracy and relevance.

Embracing an ecosystem mindset creates a holistic approach integrating development, testing, and documentation processes. Choosing an inclusive approach leads to improved documentation quality, increased efficiency, and enhanced community satisfaction. Ultimately, it fosters a strong and engaged community, with diverse community members actively improving documentation and the technology or product.

Documentation As Code

The CI/CD pipeline stages for documentation closely resemble those of regular code CI/CD pipelines, consisting of source, build, test, and deploy (Figure 7-3).

---

[1] "Pull requests" (PRs) is a term from GitHub, a popular code version control system. It represents a proposed code change or addition submitted for review by community members. Other code version management systems, such as GitLab and Bitbucket, may use different terminology for the same concept. For example, GitLab uses "Merge Requests" (MRs), while Bitbucket uses "pull requests" as well.

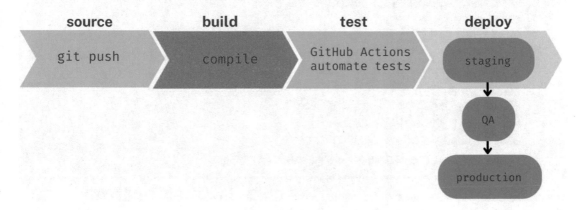

Figure 7-3. *The four stages of the docs CI/CD pipeline: source, build, test, and deploy. In the test stage, this diagram shows GitHub Actions is employed to automate the testing process, ensuring the documentation's quality and reliability. GitHub Actions is a powerful workflow automation tool provided by GitHub for defining and executing automated tasks and tests within repositories*

In the source stage, a technical writer (TW) completes the initial draft of the documentation and submits it for review through a pull request. The draft may include code snippets, sample commands, and diagrams.

Moving to the build stage, the TW awaits a generated preview within the pull request provided by a chosen tool like Netlify or Vercel. Feedback from pull request reviewers is awaited, and subsequent drafts require new preview links (see Figure 7-4).

Figure 7-4. *A docs CI/CD pipeline's build stage generated a preview link*

Next, in the test stage, the TW waits for GitHub Actions or other workflows to complete, automating comprehensive testing of the documentation and code changes (see Figure 7-5).

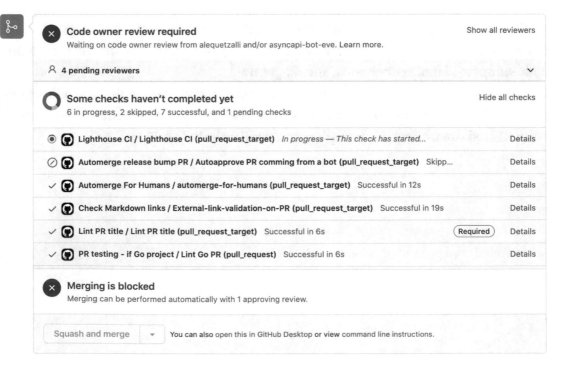

Figure 7-5. *The test stage of a docs CI/CD pipeline that automates tests*

Finally, in the deploy stage, the TW can merge their work after receiving necessary pull request approvals. Some documentation projects may include a Quality Assurance (QA) environment for further checks before deploying to production (see Figure 7-3), while others merge approved changes directly. The ultimate goal is to have live documentation and updates.

The following sections will explore the topics of versioning, reviewing, and testing documentation, providing insights into these crucial stages of the documentation CI/CD pipeline.

Versioning Documentation

Versioning documentation plays a crucial role in maintaining an organized and accessible documentation ecosystem. Assigning unique version numbers or labels to documentation provides clarity, consistency, and historical context. Implementing a versioning system in documentation allows community members to manage changes, collaborate with other stakeholders, and ensure documentation aligns with software releases.

Let's consider an example of versioning documentation using semantic versioning (major.minor.patch). Imagine we have a software product called "MyCoolApp"; initially, the documentation starts with version 1.0.0, representing the first major release. The version can be incremented based on the changes' significance as updates are made.

```
Version 1.0.0:
- Introduction to MyCoolApp
- Installation guide
- Basic usage instructions

Version 1.1.0:
- Added advanced features section
- Updated configuration instructions
- Improved troubleshooting guide

Version 1.1.1:
- Fixed broken links in the documentation
- Corrected typos and formatting issues
```

In this example, each version represents a distinct release of the documentation. Community members can refer to a specific version to access the relevant information corresponding to their software version. The changelog or release notes can provide further details on the changes made in each version, helping community members understand the updates and improvements.

Reviewing Documentation

Reviewing documentation is a crucial step in ensuring the documentation's accuracy, clarity, and overall quality. Establishing a systematic review process empowers technical writers (TWs) to leverage the expertise of subject matter experts (SMEs) and other stakeholders to enhance the documentation's effectiveness.

Creating a CODEOWNERS file in the documentation repository is recommended to facilitate efficient and thorough reviews. This file specifies the owners of specific types of files, such as Markdown (md) files in this case. By adding TWs as owners of md files, they are automatically included as reviewers for any pull requests involving Markdown files, ensuring that TWs are always involved in reviewing and providing feedback on changes related to the documentation.

Figure 7-6 showcases an example CODEOWNERS file from the AsyncAPI open source project that added a TW as an owner of md files, demonstrating how the ownership and review responsibilities are assigned.

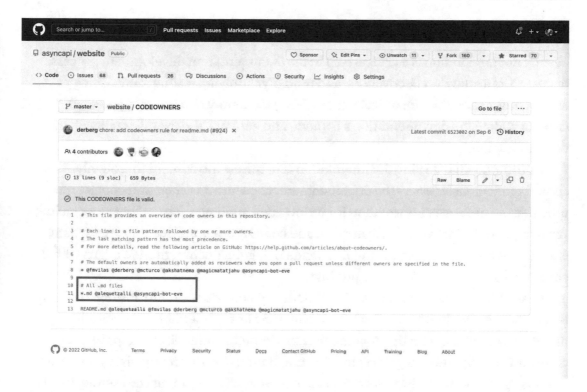

Figure 7-6. *A CODEOWNERS[2] file in an AsyncAPI repository with a TW added as a "md" (markup) file owner*

Additionally, individually per pull request, TWs should include SMEs as reviewers. SMEs possess the necessary subject matter expertise to provide valuable insights and background context. Involving SMEs as reviewers ensures the accuracy and technical validity of the documentation.

Once the pull request has been reviewed and approved by all agreed-upon core stakeholders, including TWs and SMEs, it is ready to be merged into the production branch. This ensures that only the reviewed and approved changes are incorporated into the final documentation.

Establishing a robust review process involving TWs and SMEs allows organizations to enhance their documentation's accuracy, clarity, and effectiveness. It enables the integration of diverse perspectives, aligns the documentation with the intended goals, and ensures the documentation reflects the expertise and requirements of the project or product.

---

[2]https://github.com/asyncapi/website/blob/master/CODEOWNERS

Testing Documentation

Testing documentation is a critical step in the documentation development process to ensure its accuracy, effectiveness, and usability. Applying testing methodologies and techniques enables technical writers (TWs) to identify and address potential issues, validate the documentation's content, and enhance the overall quality of the documentation.

One approach to testing documentation is to review the content thoroughly. TWs should meticulously review the documentation to ensure it is clear and concise and provides the necessary information for its intended audience. Part of that work includes verifying that the instructions, examples, and code snippets are accurate, up to date, and easy to follow. It is also essential to validate that the documentation aligns with the current version of the software or product.

In addition to content review, TWs should also consider usability testing. Usability testing involves gathering feedback from end users or representative community members unfamiliar with the documentation. Community feedback helps identify any confusion, ambiguities, or gaps in the documentation. Incorporating diverse community member perspectives helps TWs refine the documentation to meet community needs and expectations better.

Another aspect of testing documentation is checking for consistency and adherence to style guidelines. Consistency ensures that the documentation maintains a cohesive structure, terminology, and formatting. Style guidelines, such as grammar, punctuation, and writing conventions, should be followed to ensure professionalism and readability.

Furthermore, it can be valuable to automate certain aspects of documentation testing. For example, tools[3] can check for broken links, validate code snippets, or generate documentation from code comments. Automation helps to streamline the testing process, reduces the likelihood of human error, and ensures consistency across the documentation.

---

[3] Automation tools such as Dead Link Checker, ESLint, Jekyll, Grammarly, Prettier, and Loom can streamline documentation testing processes. These tools aid in identifying broken links, validating code snippets, generating documentation, checking spelling and grammar, ensuring consistent formatting, and automating the testing of interactive documentation components.

Continuous Improvement and Community Feedback

Continuous improvement in the documentation is crucial for creating a thriving ecosystem that caters to the needs of community members. Engaging with community members, stakeholders, and subject matter experts empowers technical writers (TWs) to gather valuable feedback and insights to enhance the documentation's relevance, accuracy, and effectiveness.

Community feedback plays a central role in the continuous improvement process, as seen in Figure 7-7. TWs actively seek community feedback through surveys, interviews, and community forums to understand their pain points, challenges, and suggestions. Incorporating community perspectives helps TWs prioritize their efforts and address the specific needs of community members.

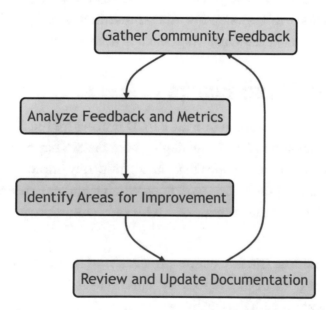

Figure 7-7. *Community feedback is central to the continuous improvement process*

Monitoring documentation metrics and analytics provides valuable data to guide continuous improvement efforts. Metrics such as page views, search queries, and community members' engagement help TWs understand which areas of the documentation are most accessed and where improvements may be needed. A data-driven approach enables TWs to identify popular topics, address gaps, and enhance documentation based on community members' behavior and preferences.

Regular reviews and updates of the documentation are vital for keeping pace with the community's evolving needs. TWs work closely with developers, product managers, and other community members to ensure the documentation aligns with the latest software versions, captures new features, and provides accurate and up-to-date information. Collaboration with the community helps TWs gain insights, validate content, and identify areas for improvement that may be unique to the community's context.

TWs establish feedback loops and follow agile documentation processes to foster continuous improvement within the ecosystem. Breaking down documentation tasks into iterative cycles, TWs can incorporate feedback from the community members, make necessary adjustments, and iterate on the documentation collaboratively and efficiently.

Embracing continuous improvement and involving community members in the documentation process allows TWs to create a dynamic and responsive ecosystem. Ensure that the documentation evolves alongside the community's needs, providing valuable resources and fostering engagement and satisfaction among community members.

CI/CD Tools and Frameworks

CI/CD tools and frameworks streamline the CI/CD process for the documentation, allowing you to automate build, test, and deployment tasks. They offer convenience, scalability, and integration capabilities that can significantly improve the efficiency and reliability of your documentation workflow. When it comes to triggering builds, running tests, and deploying documentation with each commit or push, several popular options exist:

- **GitHub Actions:** GitHub Actions provides workflows[4] that enable you to build the code in your repository and run tests. It offers flexibility and integration with the GitHub ecosystem, allowing seamless CI/CD processes.

- **Netlify:** Netlify offers to deploy previews[5] allowing you to preview your documentation changes before merging them into the production branch. It provides an intuitive interface and simplifies the deployment process for static websites, including documentation sites.

---

[4] https://docs.github.com/en/actions
[5] https://docs.netlify.com/site-deploys/deploy-previews/

- **Vercel:** Vercel provides a platform for deploying[6] websites and documentation. It supports various frameworks and offers automatic deployments with each commit. Vercel deployments are optimized for performance and scalability.

Who Owns Docs CI/CD Pipelines?

Determining the docs' CI/CD pipeline ownership is a common consideration. When it comes to enterprises and startups, my recommendation is for the technical writing team to take ownership. Their expertise in documentation processes and tools makes them well suited to effectively manage the CI/CD pipelines. In the case of Open Source Software (OSS) projects, ownership should be granted to core docs contributors responsible for maintaining the Markdown files and documentation code.

Entrusting ownership to the technical writing team or core docs contributors ensures a dedicated focus on ensuring the smooth operation of the CI/CD pipelines specifically tailored to the documentation needs. TW ownership arrangement allows for streamlined coordination, continuous improvements, and alignment with the overall documentation strategy. It also empowers the TW team or docs' contributors to take ownership of version control, collaboration, and automation within the CI/CD pipelines, ultimately enhancing the documentation development process.

In Closing

This chapter explored the critical aspects of integrating documentation into CI/CD pipelines with an ecosystem mindset. We discussed the benefits of treating documentation as code, which enables version control, collaboration, and automation. We also delved into the stages of the CI/CD pipeline for documentation, including source, build, test, and deploy. Additionally, we emphasized the importance of continuous improvement, community feedback, and the ownership of CI/CD pipelines.

Get ready to transition to the next chapter, where we'll discuss the value of *Crafting Public Style Guides*!

---

[6] https://vercel.com/docs/concepts/deployments/overview

CHAPTER 8

Crafting Public Style Guides

In this chapter, I will introduce the subject of *Crafting Public Style Guides*. A style guide is a set of guidelines and standards that define the writing style, formatting, and other aspects of documentation. Its purpose is to ensure written materials' consistency, clarity, and professionalism (see Figure 8-1).

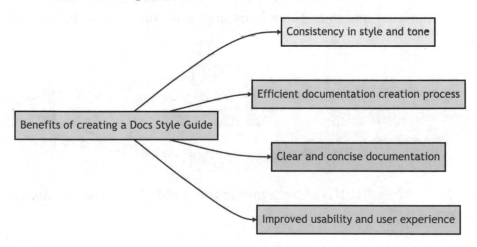

Figure 8-1. *The benefits of creating a public style guide*

Our first goal in this chapter is to explore the essential components that should be included to promote consistency and quality in your documentation. Additionally, we will discuss the significance of public style guides for both product and Open Source Software (OSS) organizations. Public style guides exist to provide transparency, promote collaboration, and establish a shared understanding of writing standards within the community.

© Alejandra Quetzalli 2023
A. Quetzalli, *Docs-as-Ecosystem*, https://doi.org/10.1007/978-1-4842-9328-7_8

Furthermore, we will recommend the different organizational roles that should collaborate to design a comprehensive style guide. Involving various stakeholders, such as accessibility specialists, SEO specialists, technical writers, engineers, and designers, ensures a holistic and ecosystem approach to creating a public style guide. Lastly, we will address the important question of ownership and guide you in determining who should own and maintain your style guide.

Why the Need?

A style guide is essential for maintaining consistency and quality in the documentation. Both options have their merits when deciding between a public and a private style guide. Opting for a public style guide brings unique advantages, particularly when adopting an ecosystem approach with community collaboration, as seen in Figure 8-2. Making your style guide publicly accessible creates an environment of transparency and inclusivity, fostering collaboration and shared knowledge among documentation authors and readers.

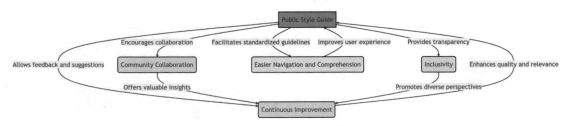

Figure 8-2. *The benefits of crafting a public style guide for documentation authors and readers*

A public style guide encourages community members to participate in the documentation process actively. Authors can benefit from valuable feedback and suggestions from the community, enhancing the overall quality and relevance of the documentation. It allows for a collective effort in refining and expanding the style guide based on the diverse perspectives and expertise of the community. Readers also benefit from a public style guide as it provides clear and standardized guidelines, making navigating and understanding the documentation easier.

Adopting a public style guide and embracing community collaboration unlock the potential for continuous improvement and innovation in your documentation. Embracing a public style guide cultivates an environment of collaboration and shared responsibility, ultimately leading to more robust and community-centric documentation.

Let's discuss further the specific benefits of having a public style guide:

- **Accessibility**: Public documentation style guides ensure that documentation is accessible to users with disabilities by making the guidelines publicly available.

- **Transparency**: By making your documentation style guide public, any community and organization can see your approach to documentation and understand how to use your documentation effectively.

- **Collaboration**: A public documentation style guide teaches external contributors (i.e., OSS contributors) your documentation guidelines, empowering future contributors to be more effective.

- **Consistency**: Making the documentation style guide public allows consistency across all internal and external documentation. Consistency always improves the user experience, making it easier for readers to find the necessary information.

- **Feedback**: A public documentation style guide allows for external feedback and suggestions, helping improve your documentation's quality.

- **Branding**: By making the documentation style guide public, any company or OSS community can establish its unique brand voice and tone.

- **Learning**: Public documentation style guides are valuable for others to learn from and adopt similar practices in their documentation.

Components of Style Guides

Both product and OSS organizations benefit from implementing best practices and comprehensive coverage in their style guides. The following outlines the core components that your style guide should include:

1. **About this guide**: Welcome documentation contributors, specify your requirements, and outline the goals for your documentation.

2. **Accessibility**: Educate on accessibility best practices for incorporating images, diagrams, colors, patterns, alt-text, and writing for diverse audiences.

3. **Code examples**: Include explanatory comments for each line of code and establish consistent formatting and color schemes for code blocks.

4. **Content buckets**: Organize your content based on designated content buckets or frameworks like the Diátaxis framework.[1]

5. **Docs contribution guidelines**: Guide technical writers on contributing to your documentation, including content selection, prioritization, review processes, and releases.

6. **Inclusive language**: Foster an inclusive environment by promoting language that respects and values all individuals. Update outdated phrases and embrace gender-neutral language.

7. **Voice and tone**: Define your brand's desired voice and tone, and provide writing style tips to ensure clarity and readability.

8. **Grammar**: Establish guidelines for abbreviations, acronyms, active voice, capitalization, spelling, and verb tense.

9. **Numbers**: Define guidelines for presenting numbers and words, handling commas in numbers, and specifying number ranges.

---

[1] The Diátaxis framework, covered in Chapter 2, is a content bucket organization approach that provides a structured way to categorize and arrange documentation content. It helps create a logical and coherent flow of information, enhancing the user experience by making it easier to navigate and understand the documentation.

10. **Punctuation**: Set guidelines for using the Oxford comma, semicolons, colons, dashes, and hyphens.

11. **Formatting**: Provide guidelines for formatting notes, warning blocks, code blocks, and white space.

12. **Internationalization (i18n) and localization**: Ensure your documentation meets the language and cultural requirements of different regions and locales.

13. **Links**: Define the structure and formatting of links within the text, external links, and asset references.

14. **SEO**: Identify best practices for optimizing your documentation for search engines, including header usage, URL structure, and alt-text for images.

15. **Styling**: Specify requirements for CSS code, font size, Markdown usage, lists, images, diagrams, tables, and other visual elements.

16. **Version control and updates**: Implement version control to track changes and revisions, ensuring the ability to trace key decisions made throughout the documentation's evolution.

Define Target Audience

Defining the target audience is essential to creating a public style guide (Figure 8-3). Understanding who the documentation is intended for shows you how to tailor the writing style, level of technicality, and content organization to meet specific community needs.

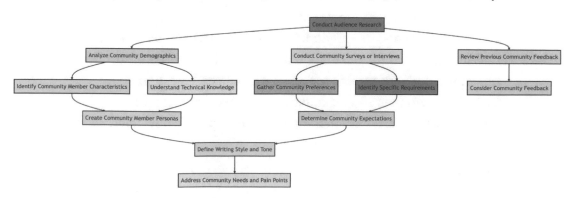

Figure 8-3. *Defining the target audience of a public style guide*

Here are some steps to define the target audience in a public style guide:

1. **Conduct audience research**: Analyze community member demographics, conduct surveys or interviews, and review previous community member feedback. Gain insights into their technical knowledge, familiarity with the subject matter, and specific requirements or challenges they may have.

2. **Identify community member personas**: Create fictional representations of your target audience based on the research findings. Community member personas are detailed profiles that encompass typical community members' characteristics, goals, preferences, and pain points. They provide a human-centered perspective and help guide the content creation process.

3. **Determine community member expectations**: Understand what the target audience expects from the documentation. Consider their motivations for using the documentation, the problems they are trying to solve, and the specific information they seek.

4. **Define writing style and tone**: Based on the target audience, determine the appropriate writing style and tone for the documentation. Consider whether a formal or informal tone is suitable and whether the content should be technical or more approachable. Align the style guide's language and terminology with the audience's familiarity and expertise in the subject matter.

5. **Address community member needs and pain points**: Identify the challenges or pain points your target audience may face when using the documentation. Structure the style guide in a way that provides solutions to these challenges, addresses common questions, and offers guidance on best practices. Consider including examples and explanations that resonate with the audience's context and help them overcome specific obstacles.

Style Guide Outline Template

Here's an example outline template for a comprehensive style guide:

1. About this Guide
   - Purpose of the style guide
   - Target audience and scope
   - Overview of the document structure

2. Writing Style Guidelines
   - Tone and voice
   - Grammar and punctuation rules
   - Formatting guidelines for text, headings, and lists
   - Use of abbreviations and acronyms
   - Consistent use of tense and person

3. Formatting and Layout
   - Document structure and organization
   - Guidelines for headings, subheadings, and sections
   - Use of fonts, font sizes, and styles
   - Guidelines for paragraphs, spacing, and alignment
   - Incorporating visual elements (images, diagrams, tables)

4. Terminology and Vocabulary
   - Preferred terminology and definitions
   - Industry-specific terms and jargon
   - Glossary of common terms
   - Guidelines for using technical terms
   - Consistent use of capitalization and hyphenation

5. Code and Technical Documentation Guidelines
   - Code formatting and styling conventions
   - Documentation for APIs, libraries, or software
   - Examples and code snippets
   - Consistent naming conventions for variables, functions, and files
   - Documentation for configuration files or settings

6. Cross-referencing and Linking
    - Guidelines for creating internal links within the documentation
    - Best practices for linking to external resources
    - Cross-referencing related sections or topics
    - Anchors and linking within long documents

7. Accessibility Considerations
    - Guidelines for creating inclusive and accessible content
    - Use of alternative text for images
    - Writing for screen readers and assistive technologies
    - Considerations for color contrast and readability

8. Branding and Visual Guidelines
    - Logo usage and placement
    - Color palette and typography guidelines
    - Consistent use of brand assets (icons, illustrations)
    - Guidelines for document covers and headers
    - Copyright and attribution guidelines

9. Review Process and Style Guide Maintenance
    - Review and feedback workflow for documentation contributors
    - Revision control and versioning of the style guide
    - Guidelines for style guide updates and additions
    - Documentation owner and responsible parties

10. Contribution Guidelines
    - Guidelines for contributing to the style guide
    - Instructions for submitting suggestions, feedback, and updates
    - Roles and responsibilities of contributors
    - Code of conduct and community guidelines for collaboration

Who Designs Docs Style Guides?

Because a style guide includes guidelines in different areas, including varied subject matter experts to review is ideal.

- **Accessibility specialists** should always be included to ensure the accessibility guidelines are sufficient and compliant with WCAG[2] (Web Content Accessibility Guidelines).

- **Designers** must be included to create guidelines for colors, fonts, formatting, etc.

- **Engineers** should provide input on code block formatting and API doc formatting.

- **SEO specialists** should review the SEO practices in your style guide to ensure they're up to date and complete.

- **Technical writers** should create, write, review, and own the entire docs style guide.

Who Owns Docs Style Guides?

Ownership of docs style guides can vary depending on the organization and the context of the documentation. When it comes to enterprises and startups, my recommendation is to assign ownership to the technical writing team. Regardless of seniority, empowering all technical writers to update, maintain, and own the style guide fosters a sense of responsibility and collaboration. For OSS projects, ownership should be given to core docs contributors with expertise in the technology. Ensure the Markdown file code owners are leading the efforts in updating, maintaining, and owning the style guide for the OSS technology. The shared ownership approach promotes collaboration, consistency, and continuous improvement in style guide documentation.

---

[2] www.w3.org/WAI/standards-guidelines/wcag/wcag3-intro/

Extra Resources

The following examples serve as valuable resources to empower and inspire you in the process of designing your style guide:

- **Write the Docs Style Guides**: Write the Docs is a well-known community for technical writers with a style guide section offering best practices for creating documentation. They emphasize the importance of user-focused writing, clear communication, and collaboration within the documentation community.

- **Gatsby Style Guide (Figure 8-4)**: Gatsby, a popular static site generator, provides a comprehensive style guide that emphasizes clear and concise writing, intuitive structure, and accessibility. The figures in their style guide offer visual examples of their recommended practices.

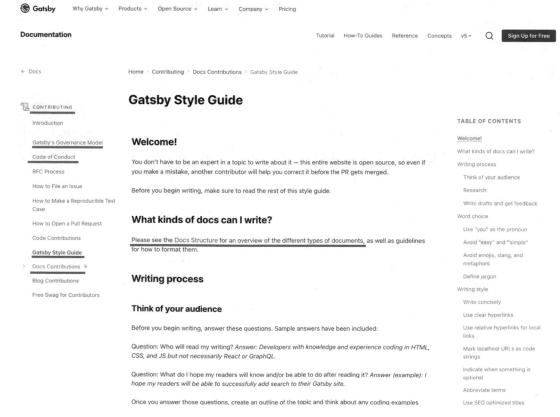

Figure 8-4. *The Gatsby Style Guide is an excellent example of organization, readability, and superb community experience*

- **Mozilla Style Guide**: Mozilla's style guide is known for its attention to detail and comprehensive coverage of various writing and formatting aspects. It guides grammar, punctuation, tone, and voice.

- **Google Style Guide**: Google's style guide is recognized for its focus on clear and concise writing, following established language and formatting conventions. It covers various topics, including writing style, code style, and internationalization.

- **Microsoft Style Guide**: Microsoft's style guide offers comprehensive guidance for creating user-friendly documentation, emphasizing accessibility and inclusive language. It provides specific recommendations for writing for different audiences and platforms.

In Closing

In this chapter, we explored the importance of style guides in creating consistent and effective documentation. We discussed the need for clear guidelines, voice and tone considerations, and inclusive language. Additionally, we highlighted the value of community feedback and continuous improvement in style guides. Remember to engage your community by seeking and incorporating their feedback into your style guide. Continuous improvement is key as technology and user needs evolve. Embracing an ecosystem mindset and involving community members in the documentation process will help create a style guide that is dynamic, relevant, and beneficial to all stakeholders.

Our journey continues in the next chapter as we explore the topic of *Managing OSS Docs Contributions*.

## CHAPTER 9

Managing OSS Docs Contributions

In this chapter, I will introduce the subject of *Managing Open Source Software (OSS) Docs Contributions.* An OSS documentation contribution involves actively participating in the creation, improvement, or maintenance of documentation for an open source project. Docs contributions include tasks such as writing new documentation, updating existing content, fixing errors, providing examples, or translating documentation into different languages.

My first goal with this chapter is to highlight best practices for fostering strong and inclusive documentation communities, provide insights into prominent OSS docs programs for participation and contribution, offer practical tips for effectively managing OSS docs contributions, outline the essential steps for onboarding new contributors to OSS docs projects, and explore the question of ownership and management of OSS docs contributions.

Why the Need?

Managing OSS docs contributions is important for technical writers to ensure that any changes made to the documentation by community contributors are accurate and consistent with the style guide and tone and meet community needs (Figure 9-1). Managing these contributions involves teaming with subject matter experts (SMEs), reviewing pull requests, editing content, fact-checking, authenticating sources, merging approved changes, and resolving bug issues.

© Alejandra Quetzalli 2023
A. Quetzalli, *Docs-as-Ecosystem,* https://doi.org/10.1007/978-1-4842-9328-7_9

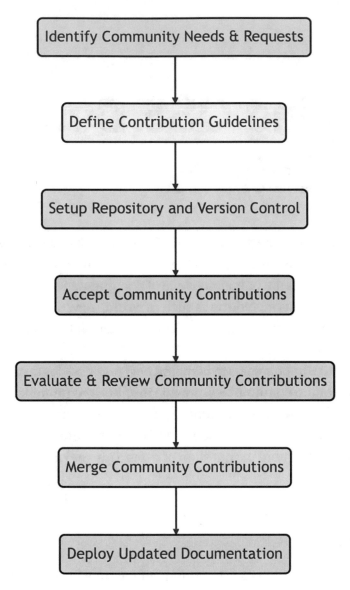

Figure 9-1. *Managing OSS docs contributions*

Furthermore, it's important to remember that OSS docs projects always have contributors with different language and cultural backgrounds, experience levels, and writing styles. OSS technical writers must manage these differences to ensure that the documentation remains coherent and accessible to all users.

In a nutshell, managing OSS docs contributions is a crucial task for technical writers because it helps ensure the quality and consistency of the documentation, which is critical to the project's success.

Join OSS Docs Programs

There are several OSS docs programs technical writers can apply to:

1. **Google Season of Docs:**[1] This program brings technical writers and OSS organizations together to improve documentation. Each year, OSS organizations apply to Google Season of Docs (GSoD) with their proposed docs projects and request a set budget to hire technical writers for the program's duration. GSoD provides a unique opportunity for technical writers to gain experience contributing to OSS projects while improving OSS documentation.

2. **Outreachy:**[2] Outreachy is an internship program that provides paid, remote internships to people from underrepresented groups in tech. Accepted Outreachy interns must "dedicate 30 hours per week to [their assigned OSS project] for at least 12 weeks of the Outreachy internship's 13-week duration."[3]

3. **Write the Docs:**[4] Write the Docs is a community-driven organization focusing on docs that holds regular events, meetups, and conferences—a popular community among OSS and technical writing enthusiasts.

4. **GitHub Open Source Guides:**[5] GitHub's Open Source Guides program is a project that provides resources, best practices, and community support for people who want to contribute to OSS documentation. They even have a section dedicated to providing docs contribution guidelines, and they welcome community contributions.[6]

---

[1] https://developers.google.com/season-of-docs

[2] www.outreachy.org

[3] www.outreachy.org/docs/internship

[4] www.writethedocs.org

[5] https://opensource.guide

[6] https://github.com/github/opensource.guide/blob/HEAD/CONTRIBUTING.md

5. **The Linux Documentation Project:**[7] The Linux Documentation Project is a community-driven effort to provide high-quality docs for Linux docs and other free software. They have many docs available, including guides and tutorials; they're also open to community contributions.

Best Practices for Building Safe and Thriving OSS Docs Communities

One of the key aspects of building a thriving OSS docs community is creating a safe and welcoming environment that facilitates discovering new OSS docs contributors.

Discovering new OSS docs contributors requires a combination of networking, engagement, and outreach. By leveraging social media, attending conferences and meetups, reaching out to existing contributors, participating in online communities, offering mentorship programs, and creating high-quality documentation, you can attract new contributors and build a thriving OSS community.

Let's explore best practices for building a safe and welcoming OSS docs community.

Adhere to the OSS Project's Code of Conduct

The first and foremost action required to build a safe and welcoming OSS docs community is adhering to your OSS project's Code of Conduct. A Code of Conduct outlines the expected behavior of community members and sets a standard for handling conflicts. By enforcing a Code of Conduct, all contributors feel safe and respected, regardless of their background, beliefs, or experience level.

Mentor Junior Contributors

Mentoring junior contributors is an excellent way to grow your community and encourage new contributors to join. Mentorship programs allow junior contributors to learn from experienced contributors, receive guidance, and build their skills. Mentoring is also a great way to ensure new contributors feel welcome and supported while navigating the OSS docs community.

---

[7] https://tldp.org

Create Yearly OSS Docs Mentorship Programs

Building on the aforementioned point, establishing yearly OSS documentation mentorship programs is a valuable initiative to provide structured guidance and support to new contributors in the OSS community. These programs offer a framework for mentorship, ensuring that participants receive consistent and ongoing assistance as they navigate their journey in the world of open source documentation.

One exemplary program that follows this approach is Outreachy, an initiative that supports underrepresented individuals in the tech industry through internships with open source projects. Outreachy provides a well-defined mentorship program specifically tailored for documentation contributors. Mentees are paired with experienced mentors who guide them throughout the internship period, helping them understand the project's documentation needs, contributing guidelines, and best practices.

Another successful example is Google Season of Docs (GSoD), a program that brings together technical writers and open source organizations. Many OSS projects participating in GSoD have mentorship programs dedicated to documentation improvements. Mentors provide guidance to technical writers, assisting them in understanding the project's documentation structure, contributing workflows, and collaborative tools.

These mentorship programs contribute to the growth of the OSS docs community by fostering collaboration, knowledge sharing, and long-term relationships between mentors and mentees. Implementing yearly mentorship programs in OSS organizations creates a supportive environment that nurtures new docs contributors, boosts their skills, and encourages their active participation in the open source documentation ecosystem.

Create Social Media Posts and Videos

Social media and online videos are powerful tools for generating interest in your OSS docs project and encouraging new contributors to join. Engaging content that showcases current docs projects, highlights community contributions, and guides on making a first docs contribution entices new contributors to join.

Host Local and In-Person Events

Hosting local and in-person events such as workshops, meetups, or conferences is an excellent way to bring the OSS docs community together. These events allow contributors to connect, share knowledge, and collaborate on projects. When hosting in-person events, ensuring all contributors feel safe and respected is important. Plan on providing accessibility accommodations, selecting an inclusive venue, and adhering to the Code of Conduct.

Find Your Community Docs Questions

Finding community docs questions on platforms such as Stack Overflow, Quora, Reddit, or Hacker News is a popular way to engage with potential contributors. Community outreach also attracts new contributors and fosters a sense of community by answering questions, providing guidance, and sharing information about your OSS docs project.

Managing Contributions to OSS Docs

Managing contributions to OSS docs can be a complex task. Let's review best practices to drive the process as smoothly and efficiently as possible.

- **Establish clear guidelines and processes:** Before accepting contributions, it's important to establish clear guidelines and processes for submitting and reviewing contributions. Document instructions for submitting pull requests, reviewing pull requests, and merging contributions. Ensure you communicate quality expectations for docs contributions.

- **Use version control:** Version control systems like Git are extremely helpful for managing docs contributions because it allows multiple people to work on the docs simultaneously. Version control makes it easy to track changes and revert to previous versions if necessary.

- **Manage clear and open communication channels:** A clear communication channel (e.g., mailing list, Slack workspace, Discord channel) for contributors and reviewers is essential for managing contributions. Open communication channels ensure everyone is on the same page by resolving issues or concerns the community raises in a public setting.

- **Designate core docs maintainers:** A designated docs maintainer ensures contributions are reviewed and merged promptly. Core docs maintainers can also be responsible for keeping the docs up to date and addressing issues.

- **Encourage community feedback and participation:** Encourage community feedback and participation by asking for feedback, hosting docs editing workshops, creating open discussions online, and providing a way for people to submit issues or suggestions.

Onboarding New OSS Docs Contributors

Onboarding new contributors to OSS docs is an important step in ensuring that contributions are high quality and that the process is inclusive and accessible to everyone.

Let's learn a few best practices for onboarding new contributors:

1. **Deliver clear instructions and guidelines:** Echoing an earlier point, having clear instructions and guidelines for contributing to docs ensures that new contributors know what quality level core maintainers expect from new contributions. Additionally, all new docs contributors need support learning the review and approval processes for new docs.

2. **Provide resources and training:** Providing resources and training materials for new contributors is an excellent way to bring them up to speed. Training materials can include docs, educational streams or videos, documented code examples of how to use the software or library, and live workshops.

3. **Assign a mentor or subject matter expert (SME):** Assigning a mentor or SME guide to work with new contributors provides the support needed to get started. This person can answer questions, provide feedback, and help ensure high-quality contributions.

4. **Encourage communication and collaboration:** Encouraging collaboration among new doc contributors can ensure they feel welcome and included in the community. Make a point to hold regular open community meetings, provide an open communication channel like Slack, and encourage new contributors to participate in community events and activities.

5. **Recognize and appreciate contributions:** Recognizing and appreciating new contributors' contributions can help keep them engaged and motivated. Take the time to write thank-you notes, acknowledge docs' contributions in public social media posts, thank them in 1:1 settings, and continue to provide opportunities for new contributors to take on more ownership.

Who Owns Managing OSS Docs Contributions?

In OSS docs, ownership should be given to core docs maintainers (Markdown file code owners). They are responsible for ensuring docs remain accurate, up to date, and easy to understand. Additionally, community leaders are also responsible for the overall direction and organization of the project, thus playing a key role in making useful docs for the community. That said, we can't clearly define ownership and responsibilities in OSS projects like in enterprise products. In these cases, the community must establish clear roles, guidelines, and communication channels to manage docs contributions well.

In this fictitious OSS project (Figure 9-2), let's introduce two technical writer contributors. The first contributor, TW contributor #1, has made multiple contributions to the documentation of a specific tool within the project. On the other hand, TW contributor #2 has focused on contributing to the overall documentation of the project, specifically the core website documentation. It's important to note that these contributors work remotely, allowing them to contribute from anywhere in the world, as is typical in an OSS project setting.

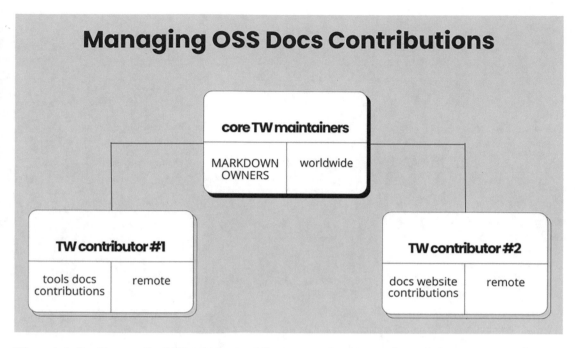

Figure 9-2. *Example OSS project with core maintainers (Markdown owners) assigning TW tasks to occasional docs contributors*

In Closing

Before we rush to the next chapter, take the time to analyze your current processes for managing OSS docs contributions in your OSS project. Think about what processes you're missing that could make life smoother for current and new contributors. Ask your community for feedback on what could be improved. Don't rush the learning process; doing the best you can for your OSS community takes time.

Now let's move forward to Chapter 10 and learn how to *Retrieve Community Feedback and Analytics.*

CHAPTER 10

Retrieve Community Feedback and Analytics

In this chapter, I will introduce the subject of *Retrieve Community Feedback and Analytics* in the context of engineering documentation that refers to the process of actively collecting and analyzing input, suggestions, opinions, and data from community members who interact with the documentation (Figure 10-1). The world involved includes soliciting feedback through various channels such as forums, social media, surveys, and support requests and gathering analytics data to gain insights into user behavior, usage patterns, and pain points. The goal is to gather valuable information that can be used to improve the documentation, address community needs, and make data-driven decisions to enhance the overall user experience.

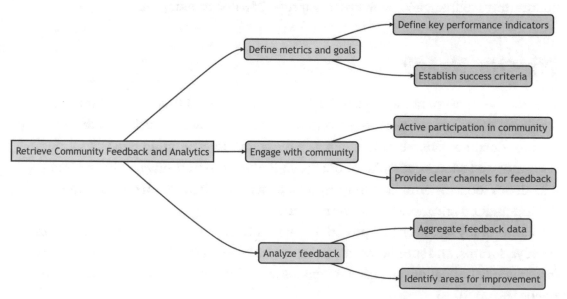

Figure 10-1. *Retrieving community feedback and analytics involves defining metrics and goals, engaging with diverse community members or stakeholders, and analyzing feedback*

A. Quetzalli, *Docs-as-Ecosystem*, https://doi.org/10.1007/978-1-4842-9328-7_10

First, this chapter emphasizes retrieving community feedback and analytics for enterprise and Open Source Software (OSS) docs. Engaging with the community and actively seeking feedback, technical writers, developers, and community leaders gain valuable insights that help identify areas for improvement and better meet community needs.

Second, this chapter aims to guide technical writers, developers, and community leaders in sharing ownership while retrieving community feedback and analytics. Through effective communication and collaboration, all parties can play a vital role in gathering feedback and communicating it to the technical writers, who can take the lead in documenting the feedback and incorporating it into the documentation.

Third, this chapter explores the methods and tools available for retrieving community feedback and analytics.

Fourth, effective communication and collaboration with the community are crucial to retrieving feedback and analytics successfully. This chapter guides communicating effectively with the community and building collaborative relationships to facilitate feedback retrieval.

Fifth, technical writing or documentation teams can own and analyze product documentation analytics to improve effectiveness in an enterprise context.

Finally, this chapter provides practical tips and strategies for effectively retrieving community feedback and analytics to improve OSS documentation.

Why the Need?

The docs-as-ecosystem model, emphasizing starting and ending with community feedback, offers several benefits. Incorporating community feedback from the beginning ensures documentation is tailored for specific community member needs, ensuring relevance and effectiveness. Additionally, ending with community feedback creates a feedback loop, fostering ongoing improvement and collaboration between the documentation creators and the community.

Community feedback is captured through various channels like GitHub discussions, surveys, forums, and support requests. The most relevant feedback can be integrated into the documentation, ensuring it remains up to date and reflects diverse community needs (Figure 10-2).

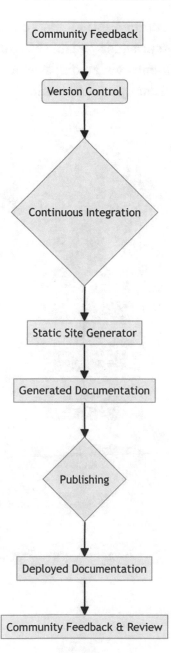

Figure 10-2. *The docs-as-ecosystem model starts and ends with incorporating community feedback*

Figure 10-3 illustrates diverse stakeholders involved in providing feedback through channels like events, social media, and more. Developer relations analyze the feedback, while technical writers incorporate it into the documentation. Product managers guide documentation direction, OSS community members contribute, engineers ensure accuracy, and customer support provides valuable insights. Even students bring new ideas. Collaboration and communication among diverse stakeholders are crucial for creating effective, community-friendly documentation.

Figure 10-3. *Diverse stakeholders and collaborators involved in providing community feedback and reviews*

Best Practices for Retrieving Community Feedback

Let's discuss best practices, strategies, and tips for retrieving community feedback!

Create Social Media Posts

Social media is a powerful tool for generating interest in your OSS documentation project and attracting new contributors. Share engaging content that showcases ongoing documentation projects or programs (Figure 10-4), highlights community contributions (Figure 10-5), and guides on making a first documentation contribution; you can inspire and entice new contributors to join the community. Additionally, social media posts create opportunities for community members to ask questions and engage in open discussions through comments, allowing you to gather valuable feedback and share it with other technical writers and stakeholders. It also demonstrates appreciation for the community's contributions and fosters collaboration and inclusivity.

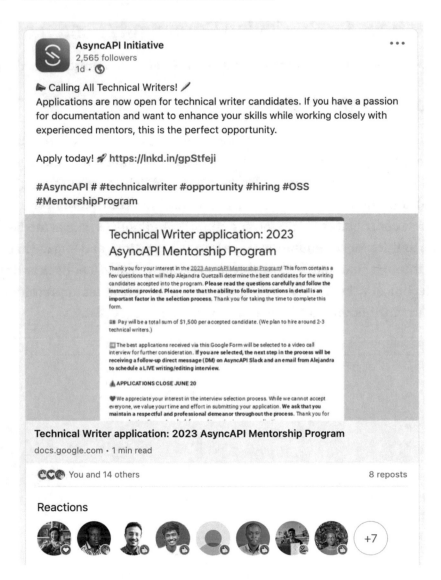

Figure 10-4. *Showcase ongoing documentation projects or programs community members can join!*

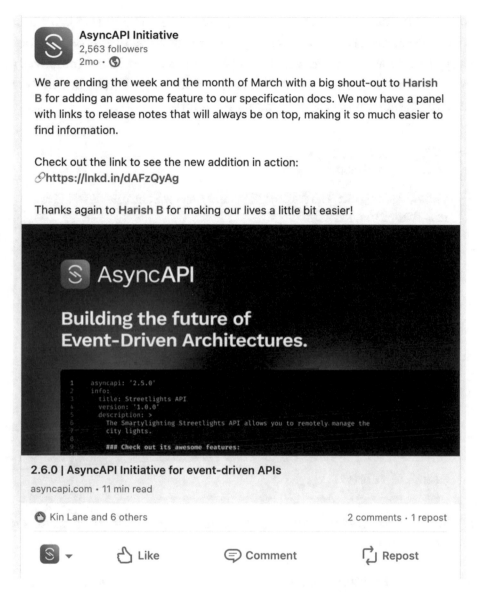

Figure 10-5. *Remember to highlight community docs contributions*

Host Local and In-Person Events

Hosting local and in-person events, such as workshops, meetups, or conferences, provides valuable opportunities to unite the OSS documentation community. These events foster connections among contributors, facilitate knowledge sharing, and encourage collaborative efforts on documentation projects. To enhance the impact of these events, consider incorporating a dedicated documentation track or organizing workshops focused on documentation writing and editing (Figure 10-6). Additionally, you can run a documentation user testing group during larger events or host meetups specifically geared toward documentation-related discussions. These initiatives promote engagement and active participation within the community, contributing to the overall growth and improvement of OSS documentation efforts.

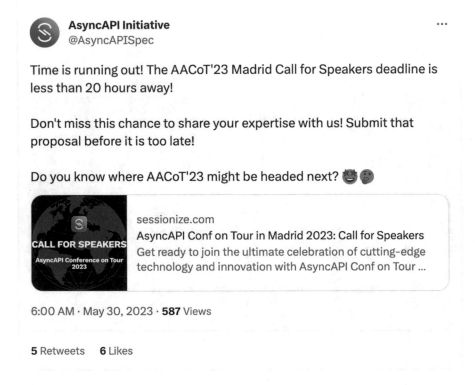

Figure 10-6. *Ensure your project's Call for Papers accepts documentation tracks, talks, and workshops*

Ensuring all contributors feel safe and respected is important when hosting in-person events. Plan on providing accessibility accommodations, selecting an inclusive venue, and enforcing the Code of Conduct (CoC). Figure 10-7 shows an example from the Linux Foundation, which executes a detailed CoC at all their events.

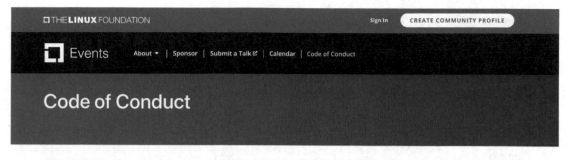

Figure 10-7. *Enforcing a Code of Conduct ensures all event attendees feel safe and respected*

Find Your Community Docs Questions

Finding community docs questions on platforms such as Stack Overflow, Quora, Reddit, or Hacker News is an excellent way to engage with potential contributors (Figures 10-8 and 10-9). You can attract new contributors and foster community by answering questions, providing guidance, and sharing information about your OSS docs project.

Figure 10-8. *Searching Stack Overflow for the latest questions submitted about AsyncAPI*

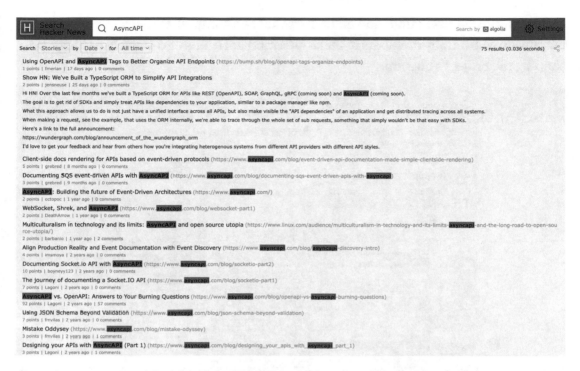

Figure 10-9. *Searching Hacker News for the latest stories and comments submitted about AsyncAPI*

To effectively engage with your community members, tracking the platforms they frequently use and actively monitoring them for new questions, answers, and comment threads are important. Regularly checking these platforms allows you to promptly address docs inquiries and provide assistance. Take the time to respond to questions personally or, if needed, identify a subject matter expert who can offer valuable insights and support. Participating in these platforms fosters community and builds trust, strengthening your documentation efforts.

Public GitHub Discussions and Surveys

Overall, hosting public GitHub discussions and surveys can be a powerful way to engage with the community, gather feedback, and improve the quality of your documentation. Leveraging the power of GitHub will help you create a feedback loop that ensures your documentation is always up to date and accurate and meets community needs.

In Figure 10-10, we have an AsyncAPI GitHub Discussion that invites the community to vote in selecting a hosting platform for interactive learning paths. The discussion presents a comparison table highlighting the features and technology requirements of two options: Linux Foundation and Killercoda. The comprehensive comparison empowers community members to make informed decisions and actively participate in shaping the project's direction.

Figure 10-10. *AsyncAPI GitHub Discussion that invites the community to vote in selecting a hosting platform for interactive learning paths*

In Figure 10-11, we observe another example from an AsyncAPI GitHub Discussion where the community is actively involved in shaping the future of the documentation. The discussion calls for a community vote to select two items from a list of five proposed docs and education projects for the upcoming year. This inclusive approach ensures that the community, not just engineers or technical writers, has a significant say in determining the core goals and priorities for the documentation.

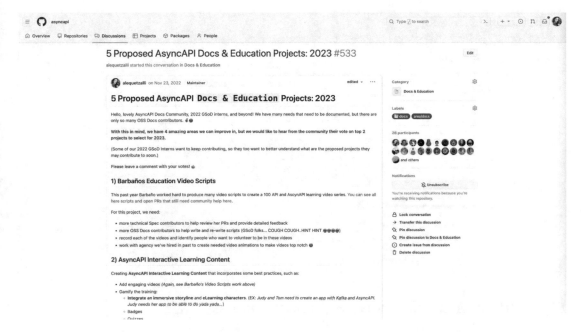

Figure 10-11. *An AsyncAPI GitHub Discussion calling for a community vote to select two items from a list of five proposed docs and education projects for the upcoming year*

Methods for Retrieving Community Feedback

Community feedback in engineering documentation can be retrieved through various effective methods tailored to the specific feedback goals and usage purposes. Some of these methods include configuring templates for documentation issues and pull requests, utilizing feedback cards and widgets, and even implementing dedicated Slack bots or Discord bots to facilitate feedback collection and engagement.

Docs Issue and Docs Bug Templates

A Docs Issue Template is a predefined structure or form that guides users in submitting specific documentation-related issues or feedback (Figure 10-12). It typically includes sections providing details about the problem, suggesting improvements, or requesting new content.

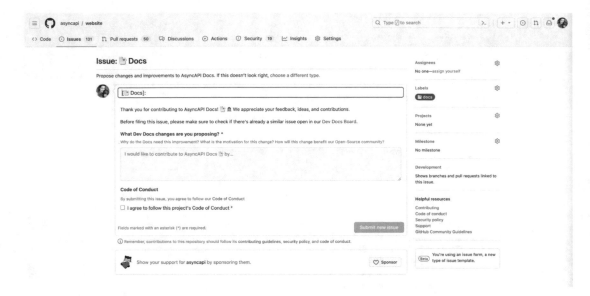

Figure 10-12. *A sample Docs Issue Template from AsyncAPI*

On the other hand, a Docs Bug Issue Template is specifically designed for reporting bugs or technical issues in the documentation (Figure 10-13).

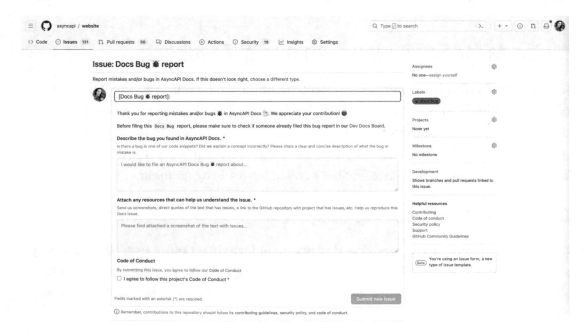

Figure 10-13. *A sample Docs Bug Issue Template from AsyncAPI*

These templates serve as great methods of community feedback retrieval because they provide a structured and standardized format for community members to express their thoughts, report issues, or suggest enhancements. Templates also help ensure consistency in the types of feedback received, making it easier to categorize, prioritize, and track issues.

Here is a sample Markdown template for docs issues:

```
## Issue Title
### Description
Describe the issue you are experiencing with the documentation. Please be
as detailed as possible.
### Steps to Reproduce
1. Step 1
2. Step 2
3. Step 3
### Expected Behavior
Describe what you expected to happen.
### Actual Behavior
Describe what happened.
### Environment
- Operating System:
- Browser (if applicable):
- Any relevant dependencies:
```

Docs Pull Request Template

A Docs Pull Request Template is a predefined structure or form that guides community members in submitting changes or contributions to the documentation through a pull request. It typically includes sections describing the purpose of the change, providing context, and outlining the steps taken to implement the modification (Figure 10-14).

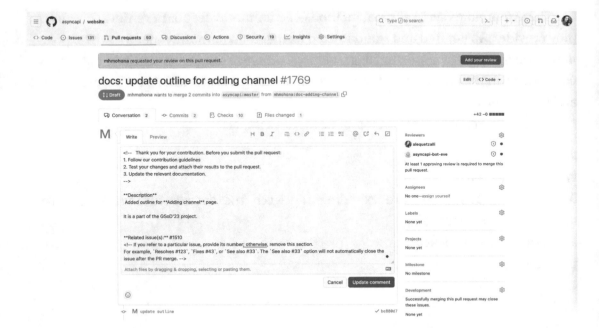

Figure 10-14. *A sample pull request template from AsyncAPI demonstrates an OSS contributor's proposal to improve the documentation of channels in AsyncAPI documents*

This template is another useful tool for retrieving community feedback because it encourages contributors to provide detailed information about the proposed changes. Using a template prompts contributors to explain the motivation behind their changes, the impact they expect the modifications to have, and any considerations or dependencies to be aware of.

Here is a sample Markdown template for docs pull requests:

```
## Pull Request title
### Description
Describe the changes you are proposing to the documentation. Please be as
detailed as possible.
### Motivation
Why are you making these changes? Please provide a brief explanation of the
problem you are trying to solve.
### Changes Made
Provide a detailed list of the changes you made to the documentation.
### Testing
```

Describe the steps you took to test your changes. Please be as detailed as possible.
Related Issues
If there are any related issues or pull requests, please list them here.
Screenshots (if applicable)
Please include any relevant screenshots to help illustrate your changes.

Feedback Cards

Feedback cards in engineering docs refer to interactive components or forms embedded within the documentation that allow readers to provide feedback on the content. These cards typically include fields or prompts where community members can share their thoughts and suggestions, report issues, or ask questions directly within the documentation interface. Feedback cards are an effective way to gather user feedback, identify areas for improvement, and engage with the community (Figure 10-15).

Figure 10-15. *Feedback cards typically include fields or prompts where community members can share their thoughts and suggestions*

Figure 10-16 shows that feedback cards can be configured to inject received feedback into open GitHub discussions, providing a convenient and transparent way to share feedback publicly. This allows community members to comment and engage in discussions and enables others to provide additional details or express agreement.

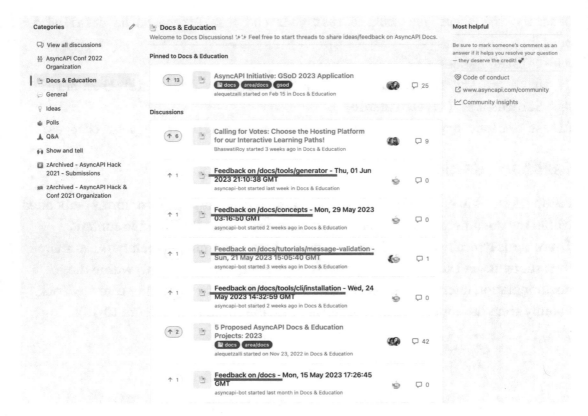

Figure 10-16. *Feedback cards can be configured to inject received feedback into open GitHub discussions*

Here are more examples of feedback cards on documentation websites:

1. **Microsoft Azure:** The Azure documentation website includes a "Was this page helpful?" feedback card at the bottom of each page. Users can click "Yes" or "No" and leave additional feedback.

2. **Google Cloud Platform:** The Google Cloud Platform documentation website includes a feedback card with smiley faces at the bottom of each page. Users can select a smiley face to indicate whether they found the content helpful or not, and they can leave additional feedback.

3. **Amazon Web Services (AWS):** The AWS documentation website includes a "Rate this page" feedback card at the bottom of each page. Users can select a rating from one to five stars and leave additional feedback.

4. **Red Hat:** The documentation website includes a feedback card at the bottom of each page asking, "Did this solve your problem?" Users can select "Yes" or "No" and leave additional feedback.

In each of these examples, the feedback card is placed prominently on the page, making it easy for users to provide feedback on the content they just read. The feedback card also allows community members to leave additional feedback beyond a simple "yes" or "no" response, allowing them to provide more detailed feedback to improve the documentation.

Feedback Widgets

You can add feedback widgets to your website or documentation to allow users to leave feedback directly on the page. These feedback widgets are a quick and easy way to gather feedback from community members actively engaging with your content.

Here are a few feedback widgets you can try out on your engineering documentation:

1. **Drift**: Drift is a customer messaging platform with a feedback widget allowing users to provide feedback or report issues directly from your documentation. Drift includes tools to help you manage and respond to feedback (Figure 10-17).

Figure 10-17. *The Drift customer messaging platform*

2. **GetFeedback**: GetFeedback is a survey and feedback platform that creates targeted feedback forms. The platform includes analytics and reporting tools to help you identify trends and prioritize feedback (Figures 10-18 and 10-19).

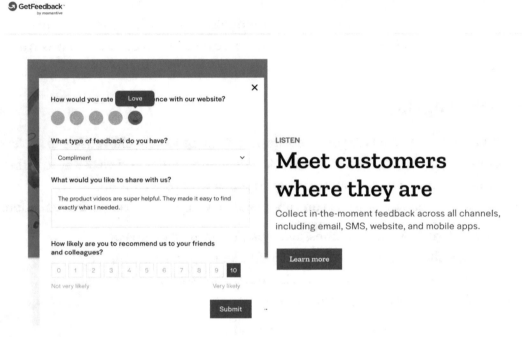

Figure 10-18. *GetFeedback is a survey and feedback platform*

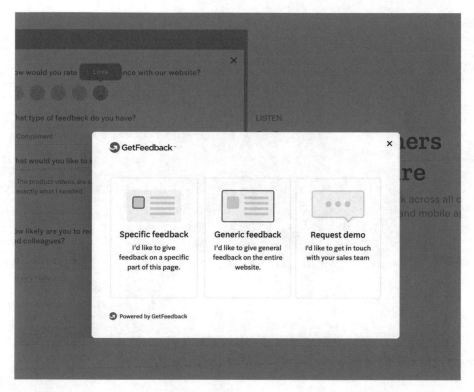

Figure 10-19. *GetFeedback offers different categories of feedback*

3. **Hotjar**: Hotjar is an analytics and feedback platform with a
    feedback widget allowing users to provide feedback and report
    issues (Figure 10-20). Hotjar also includes tools such as their
    heatmap to "visually represent where users click, move, and
    scroll on your site. With this context, you'll learn how users really
    behave."

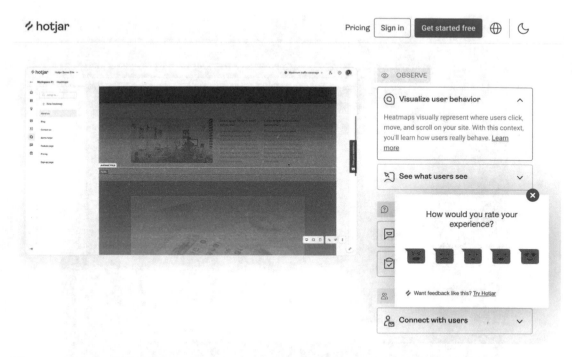

Figure 10-20. *The Hotjar feedback and analytics platform*

Slack Bot

You can create a Slack bot to monitor and alert you when members discuss a docs topic you want to track. Slack also provides an API to create custom bots and integrations.[1]

Here's a sample bot in a pretend Docker Slack Workspace that searches for the keyword "container" when mentioned in Docker channel messages and sends an alert to the technical writing contributors when it finds a match.

Step 1: Set up a new bot in the Slack API.

To set up a new bot in the Slack API, follow these steps:

1. Go to `https://api.slack.com/apps` and sign in to your Slack account.

2. Click "Create New App".

3. Enter a name for your app, and select the workspace where you want to create the bot.

---

[1] `https://api.slack.com/bot-users`

4.   Click "Create App".

5.   On the left-hand side menu, click "Bot".

6.   Click "Add a Bot User" and enter a name for your bot.

7.   Click "Add Bot User".

Step 2: Create a new Node.js project.

To create a new Node.js project for this bot, follow these steps:

1.   Install Node.js on your machine if you haven't already
     (`https://nodejs.org/en/`).

2.   Create a new folder for your project.

3.   Open a command prompt or terminal window in the folder.

4.   Run the following command to create a new Node.js project:

     ```
     npm init
     ```

5.   Follow the prompts to set up your project.

Step 3: Install necessary packages.

To install the necessary packages, run the following command:

```
npm install slackbots dotenv
```

Step 4: Set up the bot.

Create a new file called index.js in your project folder, and add the following code:[2]

```
require('dotenv').config();
const SlackBot = require('slackbots');
const bot = new SlackBot({
    token: process.env.BOT_TOKEN,
    name: 'Container Bot'
});
bot.on('start', () => {
    console.log('Container Bot is online!');
});
```

---

[2] This code snippet was created with ChatGPT. OpenAI (2023). ChatGPT [Computer software]. Retrieved March 25, 2023.

```
bot.on('message', (data) => {
    if (data.type === 'message' && data.text.includes('container')) {
        bot.postMessageToChannel(
            'docker',
            `Hey @technical-writing-contributors, someone mentioned
            "container" in the Docker channel!`,
            { icon_emoji: ':warning:'}
        );
    }
});
```

Discord Bot

You can create a bot in Discord to monitor and alert you when members discuss a docs topic you want to track. Discord also provides an API to create custom bots and integrations.[3]

Let's pretend to create a bot in Discord that searches for the keyword "container" when mentioned in a specific channel and sends an alert to technical writing contributors:

Step 1: Create a new Discord bot.

To create a new Discord bot, follow these steps:

1. Go to the Discord Developer Portal and sign in.

2. Click "New Application" and give your application a name.

3. Go to the "Bot" section in the left-hand menu, and click "Add Bot".

4. Click "Yes, do it!" to confirm.

5. Under the "Token" section, click "Copy" to copy your bot's token.

Step 2: Invite the bot to your Discord server.

To invite the bot to your Discord server, follow these steps:

1. Go to the "OAuth2" section in the left-hand menu in the Developer Portal.

---

[3] https://discord.com/developers/docs/topics/oauth2#bot-users

2. Under the "OAuth2 URL Generator" section, select the "bot" scope.

3. Select the permissions your bot will need. For this example, you must select "Send Messages" and "Mention Everyone".

4. Click "Copy" to copy the URL.

5. Open the URL in a web browser and select the server you want to invite the bot to.

Step 3: Create a new Node.js project.

To create a new Node.js project for this bot, follow these steps:

1. Install Node.js on your machine if you haven't already (`https://nodejs.org/en/`).

2. Create a new folder for your project.

3. Open a command prompt or terminal window in the folder.

4. Run the following command to create a new Node.js project:

    ```
    npm init
    ```

5. Follow the prompts to set up your project.

Step 4: Install the necessary packages.

To install the necessary packages, run the following command:[4]

```
npm install discord.js dotenv
```

Step 5: Set up the bot.

Create a new file called index.js in your project folder, and add the following code:[5]

```
require('dotenv').config();
const Discord = require('discord.js');
const client = new Discord.Client();
```

---

[4] Downloading Node.js and npm: `https://docs.npmjs.com/downloading-and-installing-node-js-and-npm`

[5] This code snippet was created with ChatGPT. OpenAI (2023). ChatGPT [Computer software]. Retrieved March 25, 2023.

```
client.on('ready', () => {
  console.log(`Logged in as ${client.user.tag}!`);
});
client.on('message', msg => {
  if (msg.channel.name === 'docker' && msg.content.
includes('container')) {
    const role = msg.guild.roles.cache.find(r => r.name === 'Technical
    Writing Contributors');
    role.members.forEach(member => {
      member.send(`Hey, someone mentioned "container" in the Docker
      channel!`);
    });
  }
});
client.login(process.env.DISCORD_TOKEN);
```

In this code, we're using the dotenv package to load our bot's Discord API token from a .env file, which we'll create in the next step. We also use the discord.js package to create and interact with our bot.

In the client variable, we're creating a new instance of the Discord.Client class.

The client.on('ready') method is called when the bot starts up, and we're logging a message to the console to let us know it's online.

The client.on('message') method is called when a message is sent in any channel the bot has access to. We're checking if the message is in the "docker" channel and contains the word "container" using the channel.name and content.includes() properties, respectively. If it does, we're getting the "Technical Writing Contributors" role and sending a direct message to each member of that role using the "role.members.forEach".

Analytics Platforms

An analytics platform is essential for retrieving community engagement data because it allows organizations to collect, analyze, and interpret data related to community member interactions. Organizations can gain valuable insights into how community members engage with their documentation, including metrics such as page views, time spent on pages, click-through rates, and conversion rates. Community data helps organizations understand which areas of their documentation are most popular, where community members may encounter difficulties, and how to optimize the user experience.

Some Analytics Platforms That You May Want to Consider

1. **Google Analytics 4 (GA4):** Provides website and app analytics to track user behavior, website traffic, and other metrics via events.

2. **Adobe Analytics:** This platform provides insights into user behavior, website traffic, and other website and app analytics metrics. It also offers features like audience segmentation and personalization.

3. **IBM Watson Analytics:** This advanced analytics platform uses Artificial Intelligence to provide insights into data. It can be used for data visualization, predictive modeling, and data discovery.

4. **Mixpanel:** This platform provides insights into user behavior, engagement, retention, and conversion rates for websites and mobile apps.

5. **Tableau:** This data visualization and analytics platform allows users to create interactive dashboards, reports, and charts using various data sources.

6. **Power BI:** This platform provides data visualization and analytics capabilities that allow users to create interactive reports and dashboards using data from various sources.

7. **Clicky:** This web analytics platform provides real-time website traffic and user behavior data.

8. **Kissmetrics:** This platform provides insights into user behavior, customer acquisition, retention, and conversion rates for websites and mobile apps.

9. **Piwik:** This open source web analytics platform provides insights into website traffic, user behavior, etc.

10. **SEMrush:** This platform provides insights into search engine rankings, website traffic, keyword research, and other related metrics for SEO and digital marketing purposes.

Who Owns Retrieving Community Feedback?

OSS Docs

Similar to managing contributions in OSS docs, ownership should be given to core docs maintainers (Markdown file code owners). They are responsible for ensuring docs remain accurate, up to date, and easy to understand. Community leaders are also responsible for the project's overall direction and organization, playing a key role in retrieving community feedback for docs. Lastly, in OSS projects, any community member should be able to submit issues, feature requests, and pull requests while contributing to public discussions. We can't clearly define ownership and responsibilities in OSS projects like enterprise products. In these cases, the community must establish clear roles, guidelines, and communication channels to manage to retrieve community feedback.

Figure 10-21 visualizes technical writers, developers, and community leaders sharing ownership in retrieving community feedback for OSS docs.

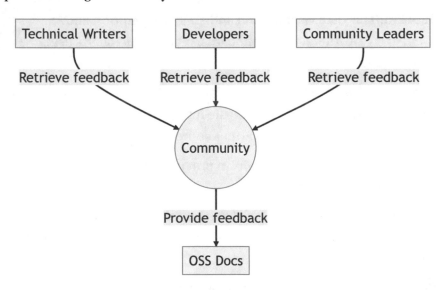

Figure 10-21. *Technical writers, developers, and community leaders all sharing responsibility for retrieving community feedback for the OSS documentation*

In this diagram, the technical writers, developers, and community leaders are responsible for retrieving community feedback for the OSS documentation. They each have a direct line to the community and contribute to collecting feedback that improves the documentation. The community then provides this feedback, incorporating it into the OSS docs.

Enterprise Docs

In an enterprise product setting, retrieving community feedback for engineering docs is typically a collaborative effort that involves various teams and stakeholders.

The product management team is typically responsible for defining the product vision and strategy, including gathering user feedback to identify pain points and opportunities for improvement. They may work with customer success or support teams to gather feedback directly from customers or through surveys and other feedback mechanisms.

The engineering team is responsible for implementing any changes or improvements based on the feedback gathered by the product management team. They may also collaborate with the design team to ensure changes align with the overall user experience and design standards.

The documentation team is critical in gathering feedback related to the product's documentation. This team may work closely with the product management team to identify areas where the documentation can be improved or updated based on user feedback. Documentation writers should also work with the engineering team to ensure that the documentation accurately reflects any changes made to the product.

Ultimately, retrieving community feedback for engineering docs in enterprise products is a team effort that involves collaboration and communication between various stakeholders.

Who Owns Monitoring Docs Analytics?

OSS Docs Analytics

The ownership of monitoring analytics in OSS docs would depend on the specific OSS project and its governance structure. In some cases, monitoring analytics may fall under the responsibility of the technical writers or the documentation team, as it is an important aspect of documenting and maintaining the software. However, in other cases, monitoring analytics may be owned by a community group or a specific individual with expertise in this area.

Ultimately, the ownership of monitoring analytics in OSS docs should be clearly defined within the project's documentation or governance structure. It's important to have clear ownership and responsibility for all aspects of the project to ensure accountability and effective collaboration.

Figure 10-22 shows that monitoring analytics in OSS docs could be owned by either the technical writers or a community group/individual.

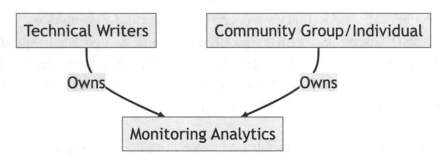

Figure 10-22. *This image shows how in OSS projects technical writers or community group/individual with expertise in monitoring analytics can own, maintain, and monitor docs analytics*

In some OSS projects, technical writers may be responsible for monitoring analytics while maintaining the documentation. In other projects, a community group or individual with expertise in monitoring analytics may take the lead in owning and maintaining the monitoring analytics.

Ultimately, the ownership of monitoring analytics in OSS docs varies depending on the project's structure and needs. Still, it's important to have clear ownership and responsibility defined to ensure that it is effectively maintained and updated.

Enterprise Docs Analytics

The ownership of enterprise product documentation analytics falls under the responsibility of the technical writing or documentation team. In an enterprise context, the technical writing team is responsible for creating, updating, and maintaining product documentation that provides instructions and guidance to customers on using the company's products. As part of their responsibilities, the technical writers may also be responsible for tracking and analyzing user engagement with the product documentation.

By analyzing the analytics, technical writers can identify areas where customers may need help with the product and adjust the documentation accordingly to make it more useful and effective. They can also use analytics to understand how customers use the documentation and tailor it to meet their needs.

However, enterprise documentation analytics ownership could vary depending on the specific company's structure and processes. Sometimes, the analytics may be owned by a separate team responsible for customer experience or user research.

Regardless of who owns the analytics, it's important to have clear ownership and responsibility defined to ensure that the product documentation is effectively maintained and updated based on the insights gained from the analytics.

Figure 10-23 illustrates the ownership of enterprise product documentation analytics by the technical writing or documentation team.

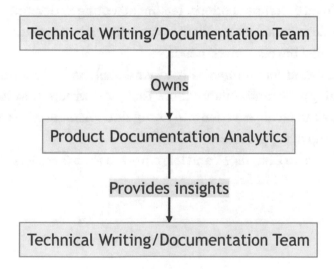

Figure 10-23. *This image shows how in enterprise projects the technical writing or documentation team owns the product documentation analytics, and the analytics provides insights that inform their work*

In Closing

In closing, retrieving community feedback and analytics is critical to maintaining and improving open source documentation. By engaging with the community and actively seeking feedback, technical writers, developers, and community leaders can gain valuable insights that help them identify areas for improvement and better meet the community's needs.

All parties can share ownership in retrieving community feedback and analytics through effective communication and collaboration. Technical writers can take the lead in documenting and incorporating the feedback into the documentation. At the same time, developers and community leaders can play an essential role in gathering feedback and communicating it to the technical writers.

Additionally, in an enterprise context, technical writing or documentation teams can own and analyze product documentation analytics to improve the documentation's effectiveness and meet the customers' needs.

Ultimately, retrieving community feedback and analytics is a continuous process that requires ongoing effort and collaboration. Technical writers, developers, and community leaders can create effective and useful documentation by working together and taking ownership of the process.

Let's move forward to Chapter 11 and learn how to *Prioritize Docs Requests*.

CHAPTER 11

Prioritize Documentation Requests

In this chapter, I will introduce the topic of *Prioritizing Documentation Requests*. Prioritizing documentation requests helps technical writers manage their time and resources effectively, reduce project risks, and foster collaboration between community members and diverse stakeholders.

My first goal with this chapter is to highlight the benefits of prioritizing documentation requests and the risks of not prioritizing them properly. Second, we will explore the tools we can use to prioritize requests. Third, we will discuss the criteria for prioritizing documentation requests, such as their impact on project timelines, criticality to product functionality, or regulatory requirements. Fourth, we will describe the processes used to evaluate and prioritize documentation requests. Fifth, effective communication is essential in prioritizing documentation requests effectively. Sixth, we will discuss who owns prioritizing docs requests.

Why the Need?

Effective prioritization of documentation requests is an essential part of engineering projects that contributes to success. Prioritizing documentation requests is essential for effective time management, resource allocation, risk management, and collaboration (Figure 11-1).

© Alejandra Quetzalli 2023
A. Quetzalli, *Docs-as-Ecosystem*, https://doi.org/10.1007/978-1-4842-9328-7_11

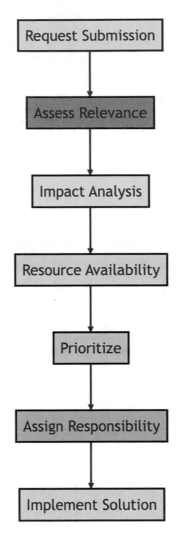

Figure 11-1. *Process for prioritizing documentation requests*

Understanding which docs requests are the most critical helps technical writers prioritize tasks, ensuring focus on the most important documentation deliverables. This approach helps optimize the allocation of resources, such as technical writers or subject matter experts, by assigning them to the tasks that have the highest priority. Prioritization also plays a crucial role in risk management, as documentation mitigates project delays, quality issues, or compliance problems. Involving diverse stakeholders and contributors in prioritization leads to better project outcomes and a stronger documentation ecosystem.

Stakeholders in the Docs Ecosystem Model

It is important to clarify stakeholders' role and importance in prioritizing docs requests in the ecosystem model. Stakeholders are not limited to external entities but also encompass individuals or groups with a vested interest in the success of the documentation, such as internal teams, users, contributors, or even community members. In the ecosystem model, involving and considering the perspectives of all diverse stakeholders ensure the prioritization process considers diverse needs within the documentation ecosystem.

In the context of the ecosystem model, the terms "stakeholders" and "contributors" have specific meanings and roles. It is important to understand the distinction between these two groups.

Stakeholders refer to individuals or groups with a vested interest or influence in the success of the documentation ecosystem. They can include a wide range of people, such as product managers, developers, project managers, community members, and even end users. These stakeholders directly or indirectly impact the documentation's purpose, quality, and effectiveness. Their input and feedback help shape the overall direction and goals of the documentation efforts.

On the other hand, contributors actively participate in creating and maintaining the documentation. This can include technical writers, engineers, designers, community members, and others who contribute their expertise, knowledge, and efforts to improve the documentation. Contributors are instrumental in creating, reviewing, editing, and updating the documentation to meet the needs of stakeholders and users.

While contributors may be employees or OSS contributors working on the documentation, they also play a vital role as stakeholders in the ecosystem model. Their involvement and contributions directly impact the quality and success of the documentation, making them key stakeholders in the larger context of the documentation ecosystem.

Recognizing the different roles of stakeholders and contributors fosters collaboration. It ensures documentation meets the needs of all stakeholders involved, resulting in a more comprehensive and impactful documentation ecosystem.

Risks of Not Prioritizing Documentation Requests

Not prioritizing documentation requests leads to several risks that negatively impact projects. One of these risks is project delays, as technical writers may struggle to deliver documentation on time without proper prioritization. Another risk of lacking prioritization is struggling to allocate the necessary resources and expertise to produce high-quality documentation.

Regulatory requirements and industry standards may not be adequately addressed without clear prioritization, exposing the project to legal and financial risks. When tasks are not properly prioritized, technical writers may focus on less important aspects, leading to wasted efforts and a documentation set that does not effectively support the project objectives.

Lastly, not prioritizing documentation requests reduces stakeholder satisfaction. When documentation does not promptly address stakeholders' needs and expectations, trust can be eroded and collaboration suffers.

Tools for Prioritizing Documentation Requests

Tools for prioritizing documentation requests are essential in engineering projects to ensure that the most important requests are addressed efficiently. Prioritizing documentation requests is a crucial aspect of managing engineering projects, and having the right tools in place can greatly facilitate this process. Here are some tool options that can aid in prioritizing documentation requests effectively.

One commonly used tool is spreadsheets, where you can create a simple prioritization matrix. Assign values to different criteria and rank documentation requests based on their importance, so you can clearly understand their priority level.

Project management software, such as Asana, Trello, or Jira, can be valuable for managing and prioritizing documentation requests. These platforms allow you to track requests, assign priority levels, and consider their impact on the project.

Agile frameworks like Scrum or Kanban provide structured approaches to prioritize documentation requests within an iterative development process. Issue tracking software, like GitHub or Bitbucket, is another useful tool for prioritizing documentation requests. These platforms enable you to create and manage documentation-related issues, allowing you to track their status and prioritize them based on their impact on the project.

Additionally, prioritization frameworks such as the Eisenhower Matrix (Figure 11-2) or the MoSCoW method (Figure 11-3) systematically prioritize documentation requests. These frameworks consider urgency and importance, helping you decide which requests to address first.

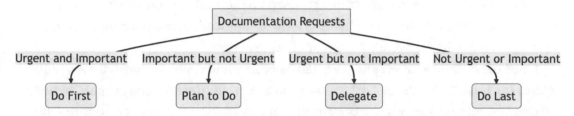

Figure 11-2. Applying the Eisenhower Matrix to prioritize documentation requests

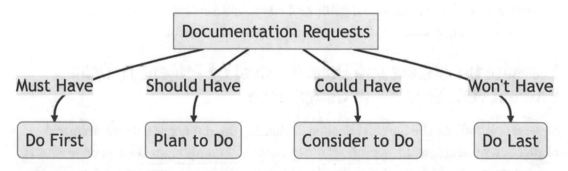

Figure 11-3. Applying the MoSCoW method to prioritize documentation requests

Criteria for Prioritizing Requests

Effective prioritization of documentation requests requires clear criteria relevant to the project goals. Technical writers should establish straightforward criteria to ensure consistency and fairness in prioritizing requests.

Weigh Different Criteria Against Each Other When Prioritizing Requests

When prioritizing documentation requests, project teams often need to weigh different criteria against each other to determine the most critical documentation needs.

There are several steps to weigh different criteria when prioritizing documentation requests effectively. First, it is important to identify and define the criteria for evaluating the requests. These criteria should be specific and measurable, allowing for consistent evaluation.

Next, assign weights to each criterion based on their relative importance to the project goals and objectives. This helps prioritize certain criteria over others, reflecting their significance in the overall documentation strategy.

Once the criteria and weights are established, evaluate each documentation request against the identified criteria. Assign a score to each criterion for each request, or use a ranking system to determine the priority of requests based on their overall score. This evaluation process ensures that requests are assessed comprehensively and objectively.

Finally, regularly review and adjust the prioritization as the project progresses. New documentation needs may emerge, and the relative importance of existing needs may change. It is essential to remain flexible and adaptable, reassessing the prioritization based on evolving project requirements and stakeholder feedback.

Evaluate the Impact of a Docs Request on Project Timelines, Product Functionality, or Compliance

Several methods can be employed when evaluating the impact of a documentation request on project timelines, product functionality, or compliance. One such method is impact analysis, which involves assessing the request's impact on project dependencies, critical paths, and potential risks. This analysis helps identify the potential consequences and implications of implementing the request.

Another method is conducting a cost-benefit analysis, which involves evaluating the costs and benefits of the documentation request. This analysis considers the resources required to complete the request and weighs them against the potential benefits, such as improved product functionality or compliance. It helps determine whether the value gained from fulfilling the request justifies the investment of resources.

Risk analysis is also crucial in evaluating documentation requests. This involves assessing the risks associated with the request, including the potential for project delays, quality issues, or compliance problems. Identifying and analyzing these risks help you develop appropriate mitigation strategies.

Furthermore, requirements traceability is essential in evaluating a documentation request's impact. Tracing the request back to project requirements provides a comprehensive understanding of its impact on product functionality and compliance.

Common Criteria Used in Engineering Documentation Requests

When prioritizing engineering documentation requests, several common criteria are often considered. Project impact is one such criterion, where requests that greatly impact the project's success, such as compliance documentation, technical specifications, or project plans, are prioritized higher than requests with lower impact. Urgency is another criterion, with urgent requests necessary to meet regulatory deadlines or address critical project issues given higher priority.

Complexity is also considered, as requests that require significant effort or resources, such as technical reference documentation or detailed design documents, are typically prioritized higher than requests with lower complexity. The importance of requests to key stakeholders, including end users, project managers, or technical staff, is another criterion that influences prioritization.

Resource availability also plays a role, with requests requiring specific skills or resources, such as technical writing or subject matter expertise, being prioritized based on resource availability. Lastly, dependencies are considered, where requests dependent on other project activities or documentation, such as test plans or design documents, are prioritized based on their dependencies.

Docs Request Evaluation Process

In engineering documentation, a Docs Request Evaluation Process is a systematic approach for assessing and prioritizing documentation requests based on predefined criteria and considerations. It involves a series of steps and considerations to evaluate each docs request's value, impact, and feasibility to determine its priority in the documentation workflow. Communicating the evaluation results to stakeholders and providing feedback on the status of documentation requests are essential for managing expectations and responding to changes in priorities effectively.

Without an evaluation process, it can be challenging to prioritize and allocate resources to different documentation requests effectively. The evaluation process also provides structure, consistency, and transparency in prioritizing documentation requests.

Estimate Time and Effort Required to Fulfill Requests

Estimating the time and effort required to fulfill a documentation request is essential to ensure the request is completed on time and to a high standard. The process involves several steps.

Firstly, you must review the request and understand its scope, purpose, requirements, and potential dependencies or risks. Next, break down the tasks in completing the request into smaller, more manageable units. This breakdown helps in better estimation and allows for effective tracking of progress.

For each task, assign an estimated time for completion based on historical data, the complexity of the content, and the research required. Calculate the total time required by summing up the estimated time for each task. It is also important to assess resource availability, considering the resources required to complete the request, such as technical writing expertise, subject matter expertise, or other necessary resources. Adjust the estimates based on resource availability and consider any dependencies on external teams or individuals. Regularly review and adjust the estimates as the project progresses.

Communicate Evaluation Results to Stakeholders

When communicating the results of evaluating a documentation request to stakeholders, it is crucial to provide clear and concise information that allows stakeholders to understand the request's status and make informed decisions.

Firstly, prepare a comprehensive summary that includes details about the criteria used for evaluation, the prioritization of the request, the estimated time and effort required, and any issues or risks identified during the evaluation.

Identify the key stakeholders who should be informed about the evaluation results. This may include product managers, engineers, technical writers, and other relevant community members involved in the documentation process.

Determine the most effective communication channels to deliver the evaluation results. This could be through email, meetings, status reports, or other channels that ensure effective and timely communication.

Schedule the communication at a suitable time when all stakeholders are available and have had sufficient time to review the evaluation results.

During the communication, ensure that the information is communicated clearly and concisely, highlighting the prioritization of the request, the estimated time and effort required, and any issues or risks identified during the evaluation.

Finally, address stakeholders' questions or concerns, providing additional clarification or information as needed. It is important to ensure that all stakeholders understand the request's status and can make informed decisions based on the evaluation results.

Effective Communication in Prioritizing Requests

Effective communication is crucial to prioritize documentation requests effectively. Communication should be clear and timely, regularly providing feedback on request status. Managing expectations and ensuring all stakeholders know the status of documentation requests are essential. Remember to respond to priority changes and provide feedback on the impact of these changes on project timelines.

Manage Expectations and Respond to Changes in Priorities

Managing expectations and responding to priority changes are crucial in effective documentation management. To ensure stakeholders are well informed and can adapt accordingly, the following steps can be followed.

Firstly, maintain open and regular communication with stakeholders throughout the documentation process. This helps to keep them informed about any changes or updates to the documentation request.

Set clear expectations with stakeholders from the outset, defining the documentation request's scope, purpose, and requirements. This ensures everyone involved has a shared understanding of what is expected.

Monitor the progress of the documentation request and keep stakeholders informed of any changes to its status. Maintaining transparency allows stakeholders to stay updated on the progress being made.

When priorities change, promptly communicate these changes to stakeholders. This allows them to adjust their plans and expectations accordingly, ensuring alignment with the new priorities.

Re-evaluate the criteria used for prioritization to reflect the new priorities or re-prioritize documentation requests based on the revised circumstances. Ensure the most important and urgent requests receive appropriate attention.

Adjust timelines and allocate resources accordingly based on the changes in priorities. Increase or decrease the resources allocated and revise the estimated time required to complete the requests to align with the updated priorities.

Ensure Feedback Is Actionable and Effective

Ensuring that feedback is actionable and effective is crucial for stakeholders to make meaningful improvements to the documentation request.

Be specific when providing feedback, clearly highlighting the areas that need improvement or changes. Specificity helps stakeholders understand docs issues and how to take appropriate action. Support feedback with relevant examples to provide concrete instances of the identified issues in the documentation request.

Prioritize the feedback based on its significance, first addressing the most critical issues. Offer suggestions for improvement alongside the feedback. These suggestions guide stakeholders in addressing the identified issues and making necessary enhancements.

Follow up on feedback to ensure stakeholders have taken action to address all identified issues. Accountability and follow-through drive progress and ensure necessary changes are implemented.

When providing feedback, maintain a constructive approach that fosters a positive and collaborative environment for improvement. Focus on offering constructive criticism that aims to improve the documentation request rather than criticizing the work of stakeholders.

Ensure clarity in the feedback by using clear and understandable language. Avoid technical jargon or complex terminology that may confuse or hinder stakeholders' understanding of feedback.

Who Owns Prioritizing Docs Requests?

Assigning owners to prioritize documentation requests is important to ensure accountability, clear communication, proper prioritization, collaboration, and quality control. Assigning owners also ensures that requests receive the appropriate level of attention and are completed on time and to the required standard.

Prioritizing Docs Requests in OSS

In Open Source Software (OSS) projects, prioritizing documentation requests is typically a collaborative effort that involves multiple stakeholders. No single individual or team is usually responsible for prioritizing documentation requests in OSS projects. Instead, the project's needs and community contributions drive the prioritization process.

Contributors may also request changes based on their experience with the project. The project or core maintainers may prioritize these requests based on their impact on the project's goals.

Sometimes, OSS projects may have core documentation maintainers or a dedicated individual managing documentation requests. However, even in these cases, the prioritization process will likely involve input from multiple stakeholders, including project contributors and community members. Overall, OSS projects' collaborative and community-driven nature means prioritizing documentation requests is a shared responsibility, with input from multiple stakeholders and contributors (Figure 11-4).

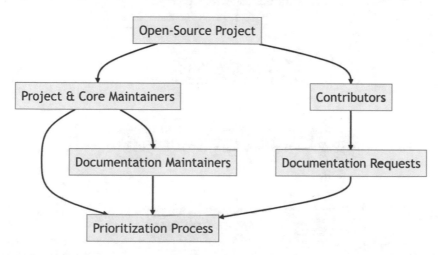

Figure 11-4. *The collaborative nature of prioritizing documentation requests in Open Source Software projects*

Prioritizing Docs Requests in Enterprise

In an enterprise setting, the ownership of prioritizing documentation requests typically falls among the technical writing, engineering, and product management teams.

However, this process may involve collaboration with other stakeholders and subject matter experts to ensure that documentation is prioritized effectively and delivered to a high standard. All of these teams are responsible for managing the documentation needs of the organization, prioritizing requests based on their impact on the product or project goals, and ensuring that documentation is delivered on time and to a high standard (Figure 11-5).

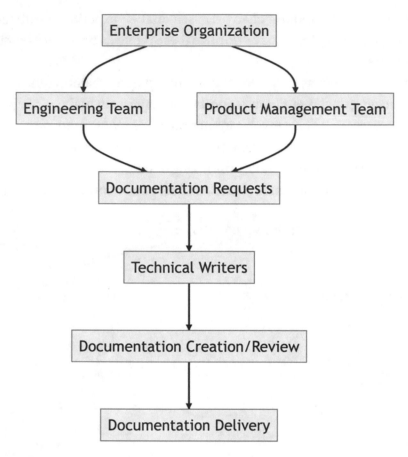

Figure 11-5. *The ownership of prioritizing documentation requests in an enterprise setting*

The engineering or product management teams may also work closely with other stakeholders, such as marketing, customer support, or compliance teams, to understand their documentation needs and priorities.

In Closing

In this chapter, we discussed prioritizing documentation requests in engineering projects. We covered the risks of not prioritizing them and the impact of documentation requests on project timelines, quality, and compliance. We also explained how to weigh different criteria when prioritizing requests and how to evaluate and estimate the time and effort required to fulfill a request. Additionally, we discussed how to assess available resources, communicate results, and provide feedback on the status of a request. We then covered how to manage stakeholder expectations, respond to priority changes, ensure actionable feedback, and properly store and version-control documentation.

Now let's move on to Chapter 12 and learn about *Open Community Communication Channels.*

CHAPTER 12

Open Community Communication Channels

In this chapter, I will introduce the topic of *Open Community Communication Channels* in the context of engineering documentation. Open community communication channels refer to various platforms and channels that facilitate open and inclusive communication within the engineering documentation community. These channels provide opportunities for community members, including technical writers, contributors, stakeholders, and end users, to engage in discussions, share ideas, ask questions, and provide feedback related to engineering documentation.

Examples of communication channels include online forums, mailing lists, chat rooms, social media platforms, and in-person events. Technical communities use them to discuss ideas, share knowledge, seek help, and collaborate on projects.

My first goal with this chapter is to explain why open community channels are critical in creating and maintaining vibrant, engaged docs communities. My second goal is to recommend different tools for managing open community communication channels. My third goal is to cover best practices for managing open community communication channels. My fourth goal is to discuss how we envision the future of open community communication channels. Lastly, we'll end by learning who owns managing open community communication channels in OSS and enterprise communities.

Why the Need?

Open community communication channels are platforms or channels that facilitate communication and collaboration within a community, such as docs contributors. These communication channels are open because they allow anyone within the community to participate, share their ideas, and converse with others.

© Alejandra Quetzalli 2023
A. Quetzalli, *Docs-as-Ecosystem*, https://doi.org/10.1007/978-1-4842-9328-7_12

Open community communication channels are important for fostering community and building technical writing relationships. They allow technical writers to connect with others who share similar interests and learn from each other. Additionally, these channels provide a way for community managers to gather further feedback while engaging with their audience, ensuring conversations remain respectful and productive.

For engineering documentation, it's a common practice for projects to maintain a docs channel in their chat platform workspace, usually naming it something such as *#docs* or *#documentation*, as shown in Figures 12-1 and 12-2.

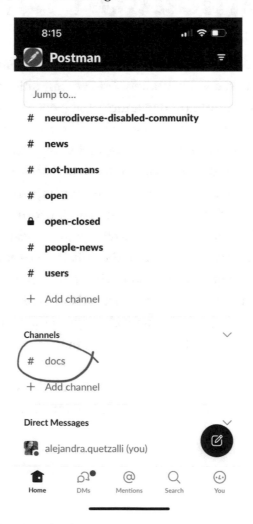

Figure 12-1. *The #docs channel in the Postman Slack workspace*

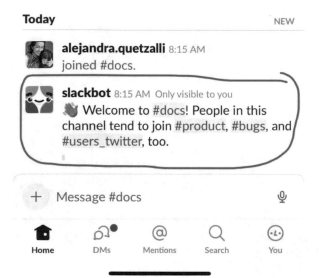

Figure 12-2. *Members joining the #docs channel receive an automated greeting from a Slack bot with information on other channels to join*

Open community communication channels are also integral to docs communities because they promote transparency by providing a public space where conversations are accessible to all members, fostering trust and accountability.

Types of Open Community Communication Channels

Each type of open communication channel has advantages and disadvantages, as shown in Figure 12-3. Remember to choose the right channels for your community based on its needs and goals. Set clear rules and guidelines via a Code of Conduct to ensure that discussions remain productive, respectful, inclusive, and safe.

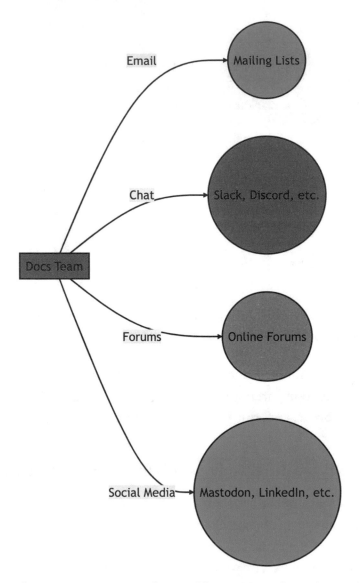

Figure 12-3. *Each communication channel has unique benefits and drawbacks that communities must consider before selecting which to implement*

Let's outline some of the pros and cons of different types of open communication channels that technical communities use.

Online Forums

Online forums are web discussion boards where community members can post messages, ask questions, and engage in conversations.

Pros

- Discussions are organized by topic, making it easy to find relevant information.

- Moderation tools allow community managers to keep conversations on track and ensure that discussions remain respectful.

- Posts are archived, making referring back to earlier discussions easy.

Cons

- Forums can become crowded and overwhelming if they have too many subforums or users post too frequently.

- Because posts are public, it can be difficult to discuss sensitive or private topics.

Mailing Lists

Mailing lists are email-based discussion groups where community members can send and receive messages related to a specific topic or domain.

Pros

- Email is a familiar and convenient medium for many people.

- Community members can read and reply to emails at any time.

- Mailing lists automatically archive messages for future reference.

Cons

- Organizing and finding information in long email threads feels difficult.

- Discussions can become disorganized when people reply to the entire thread instead of the relevant section.

Chat Rooms

Chat rooms are real-time messaging platforms where community members can converse with each other.[1] Some conference websites include chat rooms to keep the hype up during events.

Pros

- Chat rooms provide a real-time way for community members to communicate with each other all over the world during a live event.

- Sharing files, links, and other resources in a chat room is easy.

Cons

- Keeping up conversations with too many participants feels difficult.

- Chat rooms can become noisy and distracting if people post too frequently.

- Trolls can be particularly problematic in chat rooms because they can disrupt real-time conversations and make it difficult for participants to communicate effectively. They can also make it difficult for community managers to maintain a positive, respectful, and productive community atmosphere.

Social Media Platforms

Social media platforms like Mastodon, Twitter, LinkedIn, and Facebook provide ways for technical communities to connect and engage with each other.

Pros

- Social media platforms are familiar and accessible to many people.

- They provide a way for communities to connect with people outside their immediate network or geographical location.

---

[1] On the other hand, a message board (also known as a forum or discussion board) is an asynchronous communication platform where users can post messages and engage in discussions that can be viewed and responded to at any time. Messages on a message board are organized in threads, allowing for structured and topic-based discussions. Users can create new discussion threads or contribute to existing ones, fostering ongoing conversations over an extended period.

Cons

- Trolls can use social media platforms to spread false information, provoke conflict, and harass other users. Trolls can also use social media to post inflammatory or offensive messages, intending to disrupt conversations and cause conflict.

- Conversations can be difficult to track and organize across multiple posts and threads.

Tools for Managing Open Community Communication Channels

Tools help community members to manage open communication channels effectively, engage with their audience, and ensure that conversations remain respectful and productive.

Here are some popular tools for managing open community communication channels:

- **Forum software**: Discourse[2] and MyBB[3] provide moderation tools, user management, and analytics to manage and moderate forum discussions.

- **Mailing list software:** Mailman[4] and Dada Mail[5] manage email-based discussion groups, allowing moderators to manage subscriptions, moderate messages, and archive discussions.

- **Chat software**: Slack, Discord, and Mattermost[6] manage real-time chat rooms. They provide features like message archiving, user management, and integration with other tools.

---

[2] www.discourse.org/

[3] https://mybb.com/

[4] https://list.org/

[5] https://dadamailproject.com/

[6] https://mattermost.com/

- **Social media management tools**: Hootsuite, Buffer, and Sprout Social[7] manage social media channels. They allow you to schedule posts, track engagement, and manage multiple channels in one place.

- **Customer relationship management (CRM) software**: Salesforce, HubSpot, and Zoho[8] manage customer interactions, providing features like ticket management, customer profiles, and analytics.

Best Practices for Managing Open Community Communication Channels

Creating and maintaining open community communication channels require a thoughtful and deliberate approach. When creating and maintaining open community communication channels, it is crucial to establish and adhere to best practices that promote a positive and inclusive environment. One important aspect is encouraging respectful dialogue among community members by clearly outlining expectations for behavior and fostering a culture of mutual respect. Additionally, it is essential to address issues of harassment and discrimination by clearly stating that such behavior will not be tolerated and implementing a process for reporting and addressing incidents.

To foster a sense of community, providing opportunities for members to engage with one another outside of the communication channels can be valuable. This can be achieved through in-person events, virtual meetups, or other community-building activities. It is also important to have dedicated moderators who can actively monitor the channels, keep conversations on track, and enforce community rules. Moderators should be trained in handling difficult situations effectively and provided with the necessary tools and support.

Listening to and incorporating feedback from community members is another crucial aspect of managing open communication channels. Actively seeking and considering feedback helps ensure that the channels meet the community's needs and that any concerns or suggestions are addressed promptly. Being responsive and adaptive to the community's feedback allows communication channels to continually evolve and improve, creating a more engaging and inclusive environment.

---

[7] https://sproutsocial.com/

[8] www.zoho.com

Communities Using Open Communication Channels

Many communities use open communication channels to engage with their members and foster collaboration:

- **Stack Overflow**: Uses an online forum format to facilitate conversations and promotes a strong culture of collaboration and knowledge sharing.

- **Mozilla**: Uses a range of open communication channels, including forums, mailing lists, and real-time chat rooms.

- **Ubuntu**: Fosters collaboration by using a range of communication channels, including forums, mailing lists, and real-time chat rooms, to engage with its community members.

- **Women Who Code**: A community inspiring women to pursue careers in technology. They use a range of communication channels, including forums, webinars, and real-time chat rooms, to connect community members and facilitate collaboration.

Future of Open Community Communication Channels

Several emerging open community communication trends can transform how technical communities engage with their members. While new trends offer new opportunities for engagement and collaboration, they also pose new challenges and risks that communities must navigate. As these trends evolve, communities must stay up to date on the latest tools and strategies and adapt their communication and collaboration approaches accordingly.

Artificial Intelligence (AI) to Moderate Forums

Some technical communities increasingly use AI tools to moderate online forums and other communication channels. These tools use Natural Language Processing (NLP) algorithms that analyze messages and detect inappropriate content, such as hate speech, harassment, and trolling behavior.

One example of a technical community using AI tools for moderation is the TensorFlow community, centered around the popular machine learning framework developed by Google. The AI toolset used by the TensorFlow community for moderation is called Perspective API,[9] an open source project developed by Jigsaw, a subsidiary of Alphabet Inc. These AI tools scan user-generated content and apply predefined rules and patterns to flag potential issues. Moderators then review the flagged content to make final determinations and take appropriate actions. Combining AI and human moderation helps maintain a positive and respectful environment within the community's communication channels.

We can't begin to visualize the potential impact of AI moderation on technical communities just yet. A positive is that by automating the moderation process, communities can reduce the workload of human moderators, speed up response times, and create a more consistent and objective approach to moderation. That said, we must also address concerns about the accuracy and effectiveness of AI moderation due to its potential for bias and unintended consequences.

Increasing Use of Video and Live Streaming

Video and live streaming are becoming more prevalent in technical communities, as platforms such as YouTube, Twitch, and Facebook Live make sharing video content with a wide audience easier. The growing demand is partly because community members prefer engaging and interactive content over static content.

Who Owns Managing Open Community Communication Channels?

Managing and owning open communication channels is critical for building productive, engaging, and collaborative technical communities.

Managing OSS Communication Channels

In OSS communities, community members should collectively manage the communication channels instead of having a single owner. The community commonly elects these individuals via public communication channels like Slack or GitHub discussions.

---

[9] https://perspectiveapi.com/

Community members, such as moderators, administrators, or contributors, may assume different roles and responsibilities for managing open communication channels, ideally guided by principles or values such as transparency, collaboration, and inclusivity.

Figure 12-4 illustrates the shared ownership of managing open community communication channels in OSS communities.

Figure 12-4. *The shared ownership of managing open community communication channels in OSS communities*

Managing Enterprise Communication Channels

In enterprise organizations, the ownership of managing open community communication channels depends on the specific organizational structure and policies. Sometimes, ownership is assigned to a specific team or department, such as the marketing or community management team. While the enterprise organization owns the channels, they distribute responsibility for managing them among different teams or departments.

Figure 12-5 illustrates the complex ownership structure of managing open community communication channels in enterprise organizations.

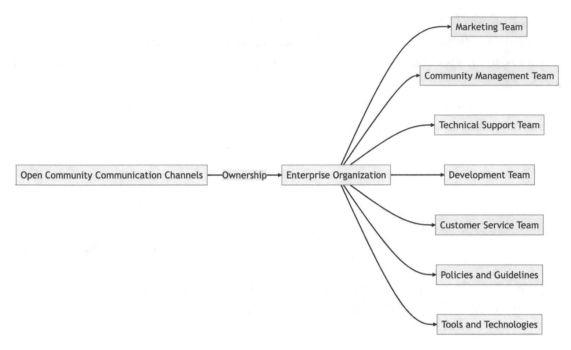

Figure 12-5. *Enterprise organizations' structure for managing open community communication channels*

In Closing

In this chapter, we explored the importance of open community communication channels for technical communities. We also provided guidelines for creating and maintaining open communication channels, emphasizing the importance of respectful dialogue and clear rules, and addressing issues of harassment and discrimination. We then discussed emerging trends in open community communication, such as using Artificial Intelligence to moderate forums, while exploring the future impact these trends bring to technical communities. Finally, we touched on the ownership of managing open community communication channels, both in OSS communities and enterprise organizations.

Let's move forward to Chapter 13 and learn about *Managing Technical Writers.*

CHAPTER 13

Managing Technical Writers

In this chapter, I will introduce the topic of *Managing Technical Writers*. Effective management strategies include demonstrating empathy, kindness, respect, and open-mindedness (Figure 13-1). Technical writing managers and leads that apply these strategies help their writers thrive and produce high-quality documentation that meets community and business needs.

Figure 13-1. *Effective management strategies require empathy, kindness, respect, and an open mind*

First, we'll outline why choosing radical kindness, honesty, and flexibility when managing technical writers builds thriving writing teams. Second, we'll learn about hiring and training technical writers. Third, we'll learn empathetic strategies for managing technical writers. Fourth, we'll discuss strategies for nurturing technical writers. Fifth, we'll see techniques and manager message templates that display a

© Alejandra Quetzalli 2023
A. Quetzalli, *Docs-as-Ecosystem*, https://doi.org/10.1007/978-1-4842-9328-7_13

personal yet direct approach to dealing with challenges. Finally, we'll recommend where technical writing teams should report to and the differences in working processes at OSS, enterprise, and startup settings.

Why the Need?

Managing technical writers involves various tasks, from hiring and training to overseeing their work and ensuring they have the necessary resources to succeed (Figure 13-2).

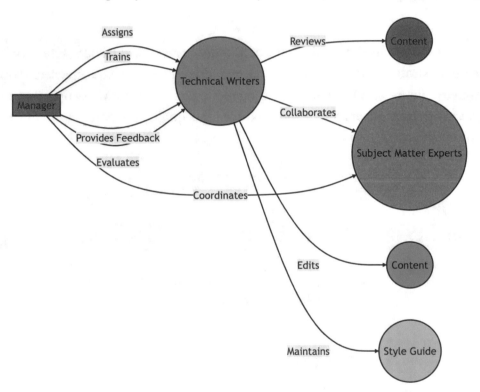

Figure 13-2. *Managing technical writers involves more than assigning tasks, training, providing feedback, and evaluating work*

Radical kindness, honesty, and flexibility are crucial when managing technical writers. They create a positive and above-average supportive work environment that supports individual learning curves, balanced development, and continuous improvement. Honesty is also essential when managing technical writers because it builds transparency between team members and management while showing writers how they can best contribute to the organization's success. To take it further, as managers, remember to be honest about your limitations; humility and self-awareness are leadership qualities your writers will inherently appreciate and respect.

Radical Kindness, Honesty, and Flexibility When Managing Technical Writers

Managing technical writers can be challenging, but it's important to remember that they are people too. When managing, choosing radical kindness and flexibility is important; be understanding, compassionate, and accommodating to individual needs.

Managing technical writers requires a balance of structure and flexibility. By showing radical kindness and flexibility, you can create a positive work environment that fosters creativity, innovation, and faster productivity; finishing work faster is easier when you feel happy, safe, and appreciated! Decide to create a safe space for your writing team that motivates them to produce their best work while contributing to your project's and community's success.

The Power of Being Specific

Ensuring the alignment of documentation with the needs of your business and community heavily relies on the essential practice of clearly articulating your expectations to your technical writers. Unfortunately, sometimes, technical writing managers assume their writers will know what is expected of them, leading to frustration and disappointment when the manager's mental expectations are unmet.

To avoid this, never assume that your writers magically know how much writing you envision they can complete each week. Instead, be transparent about the scope of work you hope they can complete and be willing to adjust your expectations as needed to accommodate their unique strengths and abilities.

Figure 13-3 shows that being specific about what you want from your technical writers involves several key concepts, including honesty and open communication, avoiding assumptions, and setting clear goals and expectations.

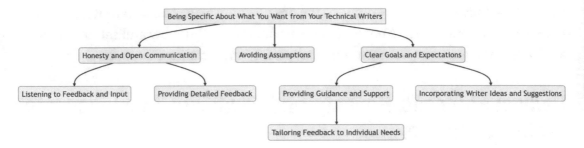

Figure 13-3. *Be specific about what you want from your technical writers*

Similarly, don't assume that your writers won't need access to engineers, product managers, and other subject matter experts. Blocking access to these resources delays your writers' completion and hinders the overall success of your documentation efforts. Communicate your preferred workflow for fixing bugs or improvements in detail, and listen with an open mind when your writers share questions or suggestions about your techniques.

Figure 13-4 illustrates the need to adjust expectations, provide access to engineers and other subject matter experts, communicate your preferred workflow, and listen with kindness when your writers have questions or suggestions.

Figure 13-4. *The power of being specific with your writing team*

Be Understanding When Personal Issues Arise

One way to show radical kindness and flexibility is to be understanding when personal issues arise. Be compassionate and offer support. Give them time off, and if this writer normally commutes to an office in person, tell them to work from home for a bit. If this writer is a remote employee already working from home, tell them to turn off the camera for meetings sometimes or offer to reduce 1:1s and various meetings to give them more time and space. By being flexible and accommodating, you can help your writers to manage life issues while still meeting their work obligations.

Embracing Diverse Work Styles and Preferences

Another way to show radical kindness and flexibility is to embrace different work styles and preferences. Some writers prefer to work independently more introvertedly, while others thrive in a collaborative environment with extroverted team members. Some writers prefer to work during nontraditional office hours, such as evenings or weekends, while others prefer a more traditional 9-to-5 schedule. Some writers prefer frequent face-to-face discussions with their managers, while others prefer an almost 100% asynchronous communication approach.

By being flexible and accommodating to writers' individual preferences, technical writing managers create a more supportive and inclusive work environment that encourages all team members' growth, development, and success. Flexible managers improve team morale and productivity because team members feel valued and supported in their work.

Be Patient with Learning Curves and Support Your Writers

When managing technical writers, patience with individual learning curves is important. Writing about complex topics requires a deep understanding of the subject matter, and it takes time for writers to grasp new concepts and terminology. As a manager, it's important to recognize that the learning process can be challenging and to offer your writers complete support.

Provide your writers with access to subject matter experts (SMEs). SMEs are individuals with specialized knowledge in a particular field or topic that help writers understand complex topics and terminology by answering questions and providing feedback on drafts. Connecting your writers with SMEs helps them to produce more accurate and comprehensive documentation. Writers require extra support from SMEs at different stages of the writing process: research and planning, drafting, or revising. As a manager, be aware of these needs and facilitate communication between your writers and SMEs.

Additionally, patience with your writers is important as they learn new skills and adapt to new processes. Learning a new tool, process, or style guide can be overwhelming initially; providing your writers with the time and resources they need to become proficient in their writing tasks is important.

Recognize Writers' Effort and Hard Work

Recognize the effort and hard work that your writers put in. Offer praise and recognition for every job well done, thank them consistently for project completions, or offer incentives and rewards for exceptional performance. The more often managers express verbal and written appreciation for their writer's work, the more your writers may feel valued and motivated to continue producing high-quality work.

Hiring Technical Writers

Determine your preferred qualifications, experience, and technical expertise, but be willing to hire junior writers. Review resumes and portfolios carefully to identify detail-oriented candidates. Conduct interviews that assess technical skills and writing abilities with live exercises but don't focus on programming proficiency; writers can get code snippets from engineers in your organization or even generate them with Artificial Intelligence tools such as GitHub Copilot and ChatGPT.

Prioritize soft skills such as transparent communication and teamwork when evaluating candidates, and watch out when candidates accidentally overcommit themselves.

Training Technical Writers

Provide a comprehensive introduction to the project and documentation. Ensure writers have access to all necessary tools and resources, such as software, hardware, and setup documentation. Establish a mentorship or onboarding program to help new writers acclimate to the team and project; assign an onboarding buddy for a writer's first three months.

Overseeing Technical Writers

Set clear expectations for deliverables, deadlines, and quality standards. Provide regular feedback on both writing skills and project performance. Encourage open communication and collaboration among writers, stakeholders, and other community members. Monitor progress and adjust schedules or resources to keep projects on track.

Give your writers space to take ownership of their tasks; micromanagement stifles creativity, limits productivity, and decreases overall job satisfaction. When technical writing managers micromanage their team members, it creates a stressful and unproductive work environment that leaves writers feeling disempowered and undervalued. By giving your writers space to take ownership of their tasks, you foster an empowering work environment that encourages diverse growth, balanced development, and individual innovation.

Nurturing Technical Writers

Provide valuable professional development and training opportunities, such as attendance at conferences (e.g., Write the Docs events) and relevant courses. Recognize and reward excellent work consistently through bonuses, promotions, or public praise. Foster a positive and supportive work environment that encourages creativity and innovation. Ensure your writers have a work-life balance that promotes mental and physical health. Frequently ask your writers if they feel supported and happy in their roles.

Accidental Plagiarism

Accidental plagiarism occurs when technical writers use content from another source without proper attribution or citation. Managers must approach the situation with patience and understanding rather than anger or frustration when encountering such accidental plagiarism. Surprisingly, many people do not know how to cite resources properly, which leads to mistakes in this area from even the best-intentioned writers.

Managers can use Purdue OWL[1] to teach writing teams how to cite resources properly. Purdue University's Online Writing Lab (OWL) provides comprehensive guides on citation styles, including APA, MLA, and Chicago. They also offer step-by-step instructions on how to format in-text citations, endnotes, and bibliographies and guidance on when to use direct or indirect citations.

---

[1] https://owl.purdue.edu/

Remember that mistakes happen; a manager's role is to educate and support technical writers in developing the skills necessary to avoid plagiarism in the future. Provide training on citation styles, paraphrasing or summarizing information from other sources properly, etc. By taking a proactive and patient approach to accidental plagiarism, managers create a culture of honesty, integrity, and professionalism among their technical writing teams.

Dealing with Challenges

Manage conflicts effectively using transparent communication and problem-solving skills. Address burnout or stress with empathy and resources such as mental health support, time off, or reduced tasks.

Develop contingency plans for turnover, sudden changes in project scope, or unforeseen obstacles. Address performance issues promptly and empathetically so writers feel safe when receiving constructive feedback for improving their work.

Assume Lack of Knowledge or Experience

As a technical writing manager, it's important to approach feedback with empathy, understanding, and a willingness to help your team members succeed. Here is a template for an informal and positive letter that emphasizes the importance of assuming a lack of knowledge on the writer's part.

> Hi there, [writer's name]!
>
> How's everything going? I wanted to sync super quickly about your recent work on [specific project or document]. I like how you [researched the topic, approached the document outline, etc.], but I noticed [several grammatical mistakes, run-on sentences, your document lacked clarity around topic ABC, etc.].
>
> I know that writing can be challenging, and getting everything right on the first draft is impossible. After all, writing is just the warm-up for the real workout: editing and rewriting! With that in mind, I want to work with you to help you improve your skills and knowledge in the areas where you struggle.
>
> To start, I would like to offer you additional training or resources to help you improve your writing skills and knowledge. I have also identified a mentor in our organization that has accepted setting time aside to support you.

In addition, let's work on more detailed feedback and track your progress via our 1:1s and regular asynchronous communication channels. I'm excited to team with you and help you grow to the next level.

Finally, I encourage you to reach out to me or any other team members whenever you have questions or feel confused about your assigned tasks. We are all here to support you and help you succeed, and we want to see you thrive as a member of our team.

Thank you for your continued dedication to our team!

Acknowledge Growth and Encourage Continuous Feedback

As a technical writing manager, it's important to approach follow-up feedback with continued encouragement and full transparency. Here is a template for a follow-up letter that emphasizes the importance of taking action on feedback received on the writer's part.

Hey [Writer's Name]!

Nice work on your research for the last documentation pull request, and congrats on getting it merged! I wanted to thank you for the progress you've made since our last conversation; I appreciate your commitment to taking action and your efforts toward addressing my feedback.

Let's follow up on one of the points we discussed previously. I've noticed that there are still grammatical errors in your latest pull requests. Consider using a writing tool like Grammarly Pro to help catch errors more quickly. As someone who also uses writing tools, I've found them to be incredibly helpful in identifying mistakes and improving the overall quality of my writing.

Please let me know if you have any questions or if there is anything else I can do to support you in improving your writing.

Thank you again for your hard work and dedication. I can't wait to see your continued progress and growth!

Address Frequent Noncommunication or Low-Quality Work

Unfortunately, there may be times when you encounter consistent noncommunication, low-quality work, or a less-than-stellar attitude from one of your writers. In these cases, it's important to address the issue directly and provide honest feedback that helps the writer realize they need to improve their skills and regain momentum.

Here's a template letter that addresses a consistent problem with empathy and understanding while taking a firmer tone to emphasize the required improvement.

Hello [writer's name],

I wanted to touch base with you regarding your recent work on [specific project or document]. While I appreciate your efforts and dedication to the project, I have noticed that your work has not met our expected quality standards.

Specifically, I have noticed [specific areas of concern, such as grammar, accuracy, or completeness]. I have also provided you with feedback and suggestions for improvement, but my concern today is that I have not seen significant progress in these areas.

As a member of our team, you must be willing to create documentation that meets high-quality standards and best serves community needs. To that end, let's discuss ways to work together to improve your performance.

First, I would like to continue providing additional training or resources to help you improve your skills and knowledge in the areas where you struggle. Second, I will offer more regular feedback and coaching to help you identify improvement areas and track your progress. Third, if there is a specific kind of support you need to thrive, please don't hesitate to communicate that to me! Finally, let's pivot to meeting more frequently to discuss detailed feedback and ideas on your work.

These expectations may feel high, but I believe in your potential and value your contributions to our team. I am confident you can improve your performance and produce high-quality documentation that meets our standards with the right support, encouragement, and effort.

Please let me know if you have any questions or concerns, and thank you for your continued dedication to our documentation!

Protecting Your Team from Narcissistic or Toxic Team Members

As a technical writing manager, being aware of potential narcissistic or toxic team members who may not have your team's best interests in mind is important. These individuals can be charming and charismatic at first, but ultimately they may be willing to step on others to get what they want, which can create a toxic work environment and damage team morale.

If you identify a narcissistic or toxic team member, it is important to protect your team by setting clear boundaries and expectations. Establish protocols for communication and collaboration, such as limiting direct communication between the toxic team member and other team members or setting clear guidelines for feedback and constructive criticism.

It is also important to prioritize the safety and well-being of your team by taking swift action if necessary. Escalate the situation to senior management, HR, or legal counsel if the behavior is severe or violates company policies. Protecting your team from narcissistic or toxic team members is critical to your role as a technical writing manager; it requires a proactive and strategic communication, collaboration, and conflict resolution approach.

Who Owns Managing Technical Writers?

The question of who should manage technical writers may vary between organizations. Still, technical writers thrive better with their dedicated team and clear ownership of their work. When technical writers report to product management, they may not have the authority to exercise a veto or make independent decisions, which can undermine the quality of their work.

Conversely, when technical writers report to engineering, they may feel undervalued or overlooked, leading to low morale and job dissatisfaction. By establishing a separate technical writing team with clear lines of authority and support from senior leadership, organizations can help their writers to succeed and produce high-quality documentation.

Technical writers may adopt various job titles, such as "developer educator" or "documentation engineer," to reflect the evolving nature of their roles and the diverse skill sets they bring to the field.

In some organizations, these teams report to developer experience or a broader developer relations organization. While this structure can be effective, technical writers must have a clear sense of ownership and autonomy.

Establishing a dedicated technical writing team with clear lines of authority and support from senior leadership ensures technical writers have the resources and support they need to produce high-quality documentation that meets the needs of their organization and their audience (Figure 13-5).

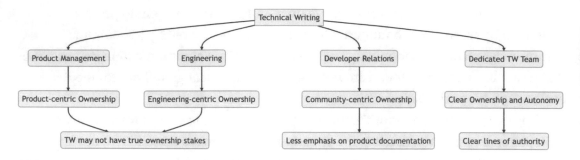

Figure 13-5. *The different organizations that technical writing (TW) can be placed in and the pros/cons of each option regarding documentation ownership*

Managing Technical Writers in OSS

Unlike traditional software companies, community contributions and volunteers drive OSS projects rather than paid employees. One effective approach to managing technical writers in OSS is to leverage community involvement and collaboration. Identify and engage with potential contributors with technical writing skills or experience, and provide them with opportunities to participate in documentation projects.

Managing technical writers in OSS requires a flexible and collaborative approach emphasizing open communication, inclusivity, and access to necessary resources and support.

Managing Technical Writers in Enterprise

Unlike OSS projects, enterprise settings involve a more structured environment, with specific policies and procedures in place. Enterprise organizations can create challenges in balancing documentation workload with other priorities, ensuring documentation meets corporate branding, and navigating complex organizational structures.

Provide comprehensive training on the company's products, services, and goals. Collaborate with other teams and stakeholders to ensure documentation aligns with business objectives and customer needs and stays current with emerging trends and technologies. Encourage open communication and collaboration among writers, stakeholders, and all team members.

Managing Technical Writers in Startups

Unlike enterprise settings, startups are typically fast-paced and dynamic, with limited resources and tight timelines. Managing technical writers in startups requires a nimble and responsive approach emphasizing prioritization, collaboration, and adaptability.

One effective approach to managing technical writers in startups is to adopt a lean and agile approach to documentation. Prioritize documentation tasks based on business objectives and customer needs and use rapid prototyping and iterative feedback cycles to develop and refine documentation over time. Collaborate closely with product and development teams to ensure documentation aligns with product releases and updates.

In Closing

In this chapter, we explored a range of concepts and strategies for managing technical writers, including hiring and training, overseeing and nurturing, showing radical kindness and flexibility, dealing with challenges, and managing technical writers in different contexts, such as OSS software, enterprise settings, and startups. We discussed the importance of establishing clear goals and expectations, providing necessary resources and support, and fostering a positive and supportive work environment that encourages creativity, innovation, and professional growth.

Let's move on to Chapter 14 and discuss *The Future of ChatGPT and AI in Docs.*

CHAPTER 14

The Future of ChatGPT and AI in Docs

In this chapter, I will introduce Artificial Intelligence (AI) roles and AI tools such as ChatGPT in technical writing. We will examine how technical writers can harness ChatGPT (an AI language model created by OpenAI) as a research tool in technical writing.

In today's rapidly evolving world of technical writing (Figure 14-1), it's hard to believe how much has changed in just a few short decades. The timeline diagram highlights the major milestones in the evolution of AI tools in documentation, noting the most notable advancements transforming how we approach research, writing, and content creation.

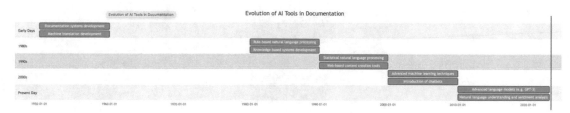

Figure 14-1. *Evolution of AI tools in documentation*

My first goal with this chapter is to showcase best practices for using AI tools, like ChatGPT, in technical writing. My second goal is to discuss why harnessing AI tools such as ChatGPT improves and shortens the research phase for technical writing projects, freeing up space to catch up on backlog tasks. My third goal is to address the correct way to cite and give attribution to AI tools and the intellectual property of the creators behind them. My fourth goal is to explain the reality of the limitations of AI in technical writing, generating incorrect or biased information that accidentally influences harmful content.

A. Quetzalli, *Docs-as-Ecosystem*, https://doi.org/10.1007/978-1-4842-9328-7_14

The final goal of this chapter is to encourage writers and editors alike not to be spooked by AI automating technical writing research tasks. No need to lock up your pens just yet; the robots aren't invading town this week to take your jobs!

Why the Need?

AI tools like ChatGPT are here to assist and enhance technical writing, not to replace human writers and editors. Figure 14-2 shows how technical writers can harness AI research tools to improve personal efficiency, leading to fewer backlog tasks and happy writers.

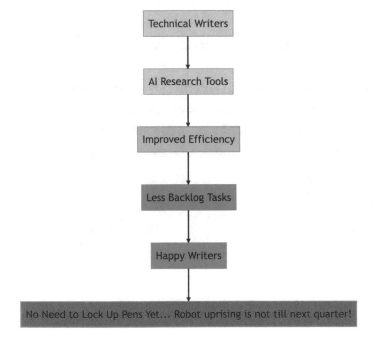

Figure 14-2. *Integrating AI tools into technical writing*

The future of ChatGPT and AI in docs is promising and exciting, as it opens up the field for junior technical writers, makes research faster, and even recommends new angles to explore in your writing. With these advances, technical writing jobs can change to focus more on editing and community building.

In today's fast-paced business environment, businesses always seek ways to increase efficiency and productivity. Some companies will see the rise of AI tools in documentation as an opportunity to eliminate roles, but balanced teams will view AI as a tool that helps writers catch up with the workload and backlog tasks.

Technical writing teams always feel like they need writers! Instead of eliminating roles, AI can automate tasks that save time, enabling the current team member to focus on more important tasks such as editing and community building. By using AI tools to increase productivity, teams can finally cope with the workload without sacrificing quality or efficiency. The benefits of AI tools in engineering documentation are clear: they automate tasks, save time, and empower teams to work more efficiently and effectively. These AI tools also produce detailed and structured content written by a subject matter expert and inspire new ideas for writers during their editing process.

The future is here; rather than fearing job loss to the robots, it's time to learn how to harness AI for our benefit. Future, here we come!

Opens the Field for Juniors

One of the most significant benefits of AI in documentation is that it opens opportunities for junior technical writers. With AI tools available to help with research and writing, juniors can finally contribute to documentation projects in ways that were impossible before. Creating a more inclusive and diverse team brings fresh perspectives and ideas.

In addition to the significant benefits of AI in documentation opening opportunities for junior technical writers, it also levels the playing field for them regarding access to knowledge and experience. In many cases, senior technical writers and SMEs may not have time to work closely with juniors or provide them with extensive guidance and training. However, with AI tools available to assist with research and writing, juniors can rely less on the guidance of senior team members and contribute more independently to documentation projects (Figure 14-3).

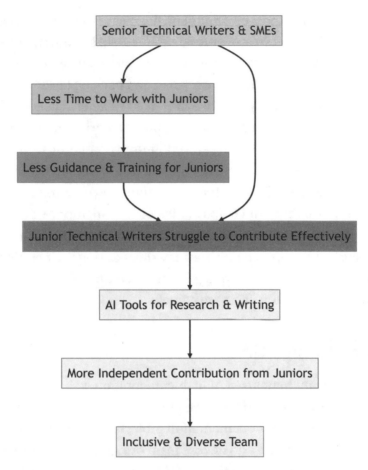

Figure 14-3. *AI tools open opportunities for junior technical writers*

Accelerates Research Process

Harnessing AI tools such as ChatGPT has the potential to greatly improve and shorten the research phase for technical writing projects while also freeing up space to catch up on backlog tasks.

One of the main benefits of using AI tools like ChatGPT for research is that they can quickly analyze vast amounts of data and extract the most relevant information. Reducing the time and effort required for manual research and data analysis allows technical writers to focus on more important tasks. Not to mention, ChatGPT and other AI tools can also suggest new angles and topics for technical writing projects, leading to greater creativity and innovation in content creation.

Using AI to automate certain parts of the writing process empowers technical writers to focus on producing better content and catching up on backlog tasks.

Jobs Change to Editing and Community-Building Focus

As with any new technology, technical writers are concerned about job security. However, balanced teams view AI as a tool that helps them catch up with the workload rather than a reason to eliminate roles. AI saves time by automating tasks, allowing writers to shift focus onto more important tasks such as editing and community building. Figure 14-4 illustrates how harnessing AI tools in technical writing allows writers to focus more on editing and community building.

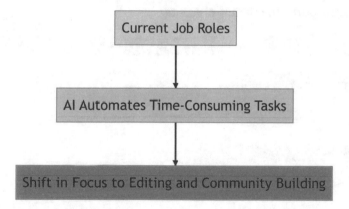

Figure 14-4. *Harnessing AI tools in technical writing*

Cite and Give Attribution to ChatGPT and AI Tools

Using AI tools like ChatGPT to generate information or content is not inherently plagiarism. However, technical writers must properly cite and attribute content generated by AI tools; they cannot copy and paste AI content directly into their documentation without proper context or resource citation.

One way to give attribution to AI tools is to include a citation in the footnotes or endnotes of the document, stating the source of information generated by the AI tool. When citing AI tools like ChatGPT, technical writers can provide attribution by mentioning the tool's name, such as "ChatGPT," and include the source (e.g., OpenAI). Providing proper citations helps acknowledge the contributions of AI tools and ensures transparency and credibility in the documentation.

For example, a technical writer could include a note that reads: "The following code snippet was generated using OpenAI's ChatGPT AI language model."

Fact-Checking AI: Understanding Limitations and Potential Risks of ChatGPT and AI Tools

One of the main issues with AI language models is that they can generate biased or incorrect information, leading to potentially harmful consequences. For example, in 2020, OpenAI released an update to its GPT-3 language model that could produce racist, sexist, and other harmful content. Fact-checking AI is essential in addressing these limitations and potential risks. Figure 14-5 compares the benefits and limitations of AI and highlights the importance of fact-checking.

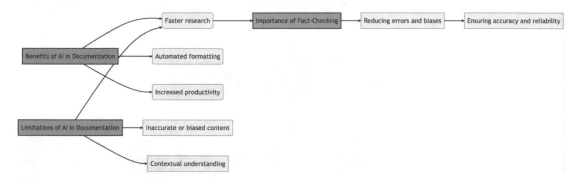

Figure 14-5. *Benefits and limitations of AI and the importance of fact-checking*

Technical writers must review and verify the accuracy of the information produced by the model. Fact-checking identifies errors, biases, and inaccuracies. By addressing these issues, we can continue using AI to enhance our lives while minimizing potential harm.

Who Owns Fact-Checking AI Resources?

The responsibility for fact-checking content sourced from AI tools like ChatGPT falls on the technical writer. Technical writers must be diligent in verifying the information generated by AI tools; it's important to conduct a thorough editorial review of all final documentation to ensure accuracy and completeness.

Technical writers must also know the potential legal and ethical implications of using AI tools for documentation. For example, if an AI-generated document contains false or misleading information, the company or organization responsible for publishing it could face legal or reputational consequences. While AI tools like ChatGPT can enhance the documentation process, they also require careful management and oversight to ensure accuracy, completeness, and ethical compliance.

Figure 14-6 illustrates a technical writer's responsibility to fact-check content sourced from AI tools.

Figure 14-6. *A technical writer's responsibility is to fact-check all content sourced from AI tools*

More Resources

Some studies and articles explore AI's potential impacts on job roles in various industries, including technical writing:

- "AI and the Future of Technical Writing" by Ray Gallon and John O'Duinn (2018)

- "The Impact of AI on Technical Communication" by Paul Wlodarczyk (2020)

- "AI and Technical Communication: Opportunities, Risks, and Responsibilities" by Kirk St. Amant and Beverly E. Woolf (2019)

- "The Future of Work: How New Technologies Are Transforming Tasks" by McKinsey Global Institute (2018)

In Closing

In this chapter, we learned why ChatGPT and AI represent an exciting new frontier for technical writers, potentially revolutionizing how we approach the documentation creation process. We also detailed how AI tools open the doors for junior technical writers in the field and how technical writing jobs are shifting to more editorial and community-building work. We also discussed why AI tools shouldn't replace technical writers but boost their work processes. Organizations need technical writers to fact-check information generated by AI tools and rewrite content that meets community needs.

A Parting Poem

Here is a poem ChatGPT generated inspired by prompts from the docs-as-ecosystem model. Enjoy!

Amidst the world of tech and code,

Where documentation is oft bestowed,

There lies a truth we can't ignore,

Docs are an ongoing conversation, not a chore.

With each new version and release,

Users look for guidance and peace,

And that's where community comes into play,

A collaborative effort to pave the way.

In the world of engineering, where complexity reigns,

Docs-as-ecosystem offers clarity, untangling the chains.

With community-centric focus and collaborative care,

Technical writing becomes a tool to help projects dare.

As users navigate through the digital maze,

Docs that are intuitive become a welcome phase.

Engaging the community and their feedback in tow,

Is the key to building docs that truly glow.

With every contribution, the ecosystem thrives,

And the documentation grows, reaching new heights.

No longer just a collection of static files,

But a living, breathing, interactive guide.[1]

---

[1] ChatGPT (2023). Docs-as-ecosystem: a community-centric approach to engineering docs [poem]. Inspired by the prompts "docs-as-ecosystem," "docs are an ongoing conversation," and "community-centric approach to engineering docs."

Index

A

Accessibility
- ambiguous/incomplete anchor text, 7, 8
- audits, documentation, 1
- blinking/flashing content, 8, 9
- color-blind-friendly palettes, 9, 10
- documentation steps, 4–6
- duplicate alt-text, 11
- duplicate form labels, 12–14
- Empty Heading Tag, 14
- Empty Links, 15
- empty/missing table headers, 16, 17
- font sizes, 20
- free screen reader, 21
- Image Missing Alternative Text, 17
- Incorrect Heading Order, 17
- Insufficient Color Contrast, 17
- Justified Text, 20
- Missing Language Declaration, 18
- missing transcript, 19
- moving content, 19
- need, 1–4
- Semantic HTML, 6
- testing tools, 21

Accessible carousel, 19
Alt tags, 45
Analytics platforms, 178
- Adobe Analytics, 179
- Clicky, 179
- Google Analytics 4 (GA4), 179
- IBM Watson Analytics, 179
- Kissmetrics, 179
- metrics, 178
- Mixpanel, 179
- Piwik, 179
- Power BI, 179
- SEMrush, 180
- Tableau, 179

Anchor text, 44
API documentation process, 85, 86, 93, 101, 102
- action, 89
- AsyncAPI Studio, 98
- documenting GraphQL APIs, 101
- error message, 96
- features, 87, 89
- overview, 88
- Postman, 97
- requests and responses, 90
- structuring, 87
- SwaggerHub, 99
- test, 96
- tools for testing, 97
- tutorials, 100
- value, 87
- version, 91
- writing API documentation, 101

API's authentication process, 93
Artificial Intelligence (AI), 225
- aim, 53
- ML, search algorithms, 53
- NLP, 53, 54
- search engines, 54, 55

Printed in the United States
by Baker & Taylor Publisher Services